Owner-Occupied Property Financing with SBA Mortgage Loans

How to Use SBA Mortgage Programs to Buy or Refinance Your Business Property

By Joseph G. Correa

Licensed Mortgage Broker, Finibi Mortgage

Copyright & Legal Notice

Published by Live Stronger Faster

The information provided in this book is for educational and informational purposes only and does not constitute financial, legal, tax, or investment advice. Although the author is a licensed mortgage professional, the content presented is general in nature and is not intended as personalized guidance for any specific individual, business, or financial situation.

The strategies, loan structures, and examples discussed in this book are illustrative and educational in nature. They are intended to demonstrate concepts related to SBA commercial mortgage financing, including SBA 7(a) and 504 loan programs, borrower qualification, debt service coverage analysis, property acquisition, refinancing, construction financing, and advanced loan structuring. These examples do not represent guaranteed approvals, loan terms, or outcomes. Results may vary significantly based on individual financial profiles, credit history, business performance, property type, market conditions, and lender-specific guidelines.

SBA loan programs are subject to eligibility requirements, regulatory guidelines, and changes established by the U.S. Small Business Administration and participating lenders. Borrowers are encouraged to consult directly with qualified financial, legal, and tax professionals before making any financing or investment decisions.

The author and publisher make no representations or warranties regarding the accuracy, completeness, or applicability of the content and disclaim any liability for errors, omissions, or outcomes resulting from the use or misuse of the information contained in this book.

First Edition, 2026

Table of Contents

Introduction

In the journey of building a business, there comes a pivotal moment when renting no longer makes sense and ownership becomes the strategic next step. That moment represents more than just a financial decision—it signals a shift in mindset, a commitment to long-term stability, and a move toward building real wealth. Owner-occupied commercial real estate is one of the most powerful tools available to entrepreneurs, yet it remains one of the most misunderstood opportunities in the business world. Many business owners continue to lease their space year after year, unknowingly leaving behind equity, tax advantages, and control that could transform their financial future. This book is designed to change that. It will show you exactly how to use SBA mortgage financing to take ownership of your business property, reduce long-term costs, and position yourself for sustainable growth.

Owner-occupied property financing through SBA mortgage programs offers a unique advantage that traditional commercial loans often cannot match. Unlike investor-focused loans that prioritize cash flow from tenants, SBA loans are specifically structured to support business owners who want to operate from their own property. This means more flexible underwriting, lower down payment requirements, longer terms, and, in many cases, significantly lower monthly payments. For many entrepreneurs, this is the bridge between renting and owning—a bridge that can be crossed with far less capital than they initially believed. The key is understanding how these programs work, how lenders evaluate your business, and how to position yourself as a strong borrower.

One of the most important concepts you will learn in this book is the definition of "owner-occupied" within SBA financing. In general, SBA guidelines require that the business occupy at least 51% of the property for existing buildings, or 60% for new construction. This requirement is what distinguishes these loans from investment property financing and is also what allows for more favorable terms. The SBA's mission is to support small businesses, and by financing owner-occupied properties, they are helping business owners build equity while strengthening their operations. This creates a powerful alignment between the borrower, the lender, and the broader economy.

As you move through this book, you will begin to see how owning your business property can dramatically change your financial trajectory. Instead of paying rent to a landlord, you are paying down a loan that builds equity in an asset you control. Over time, this equity can become a significant source of wealth. It can be leveraged for expansion, used as collateral for additional financing, or even sold as part of a larger exit strategy. In many cases, the property itself becomes just as valuable as the business operating within it. This dual-asset strategy—owning both the business and the real estate—is one of the most effective ways to create long-term financial security.

Another key advantage of owner-occupied SBA financing is stability. Rent can increase unpredictably, leases can expire at inconvenient times, and landlords can make decisions that impact your operations. When you own your property, you eliminate many of these uncertainties. You gain control over your environment, your costs, and your future. This stability allows you to focus on growing your business rather than reacting to external pressures. It also provides a sense of permanence that can enhance your brand, improve customer perception, and strengthen your position in the market.

However, transitioning from leasing to owning is not simply a matter of finding a property and applying for a loan. It requires a strategic approach, a clear understanding of your financials, and careful planning. Lenders will evaluate your business income, your credit profile, your experience, and your ability to repay the loan. They will also assess the property itself, including its value, condition, and suitability for your business. This process can seem complex, but with the right knowledge and preparation, it becomes manageable—and even predictable.

Throughout this book, you will learn how to navigate each step of this process with confidence. You will discover how to determine whether owning is the right move for your business, how to identify properties that meet SBA requirements, and how to structure your loan for maximum benefit. You will also learn how to present your financials in a way that strengthens your application, how to avoid common mistakes that lead to denials, and how to work effectively with lenders, brokers, and other professionals involved in the transaction.

One of the most powerful shifts you will experience is in how you view your business expenses. Rent is often seen as a necessary cost of doing business, but when you begin to analyze it from a long-term perspective, it becomes clear that it is also a missed opportunity. Every rent payment is money that does not build equity, does not create ownership, and does not contribute to your long-term wealth. By contrast, mortgage payments—especially under SBA programs—are structured to gradually transfer ownership to you. Over time, this transforms what was once an expense into an investment.

In addition to equity growth, owner-occupied properties offer potential tax advantages. While tax strategies should always be discussed with a qualified professional, many business owners benefit from deductions related to mortgage interest, depreciation, and operating expenses. These advantages can further reduce the effective cost of ownership, making it even more attractive compared to leasing. When combined with stable payments and long-term appreciation, the financial benefits of ownership become increasingly compelling.

Another important aspect of SBA owner-occupied financing is flexibility. These loans can be used for a wide range of property types, including office buildings, retail spaces, warehouses, medical facilities, and more. Whether you are a service-based business, a retailer, or a manufacturer, there is likely an SBA financing solution that fits your needs. Additionally, these programs can be used not only for purchases but also for refinancing existing debt, allowing you to restructure your finances and improve cash flow.

As you continue reading, you will also gain insight into how to think like a lender. Understanding the lender's perspective is one of the most valuable skills you can develop. Lenders are not simply looking at numbers; they are evaluating risk, consistency, and the overall strength of your business. By learning what they prioritize and how they make decisions, you can position yourself more effectively and increase your chances of approval. This knowledge transforms the loan process from a mystery into a strategic exercise.

This book is not just about obtaining a loan—it is about using that loan as a tool for growth. Owner-occupied property financing is a foundation that can support expansion, improve operational efficiency, and create new opportunities. For example, owning your space may allow you to customize it to better serve your customers, increase capacity, or add new services. It may also provide additional space that can be leased to other tenants, creating an additional income stream. These possibilities highlight the versatility of commercial real estate as both an operational asset and an investment.

You will also learn how timing plays a critical role in this process. The decision to buy should align with your business's financial health, growth trajectory, and long-term goals. Entering into ownership too early or without proper preparation can create challenges, while waiting too long can result in missed opportunities. By understanding the indicators that signal readiness—such as consistent income, strong cash flow, and a clear business plan—you can make informed decisions that support your success.

Throughout this journey, mindset is just as important as strategy. Many business owners hesitate to pursue ownership because they believe it is out of reach or too complicated. This book is designed to break down those barriers and show you that, with the right approach, ownership is not only achievable but also highly advantageous. It will challenge you to think bigger, plan more strategically, and take control of your financial future.

As part of The SBA Commercial Mortgage Loan Mastery Series, this book builds on the foundational knowledge established in the earlier volumes and prepares you for more advanced strategies in the books that follow. Each book in this series is designed to guide you step by step, from understanding the basics to mastering complex deal structures. By the time you complete this series, you will have a comprehensive understanding of how to use SBA mortgage financing to build, scale, and optimize your business and real estate portfolio.

Owner-occupied property financing is more than a transaction—it is a transformation. It changes how you view your business, your finances, and your future. It allows you to move from paying for space to owning it, from short-term thinking to long-term planning, and from uncertainty to control. This book will give you the tools, insights, and confidence to make that transformation successfully.

As you begin this journey, keep in mind that every successful business owner who owns their property started at the same place you are now—with questions, uncertainties, and a desire to grow. The difference is that they took action, educated themselves, and leveraged the opportunities available to them. Now it is your turn.

Chapter 1

Understanding Owner-Occupied SBA Mortgage Financing

The concept of owner-occupied commercial real estate financing through SBA mortgage programs represents one of the most powerful yet underutilized wealth-building strategies available to business owners today. At its core, owner-occupied financing allows a business owner to purchase or refinance a property that their business will primarily occupy and operate from. Instead of paying rent to a landlord, the business becomes both the tenant and the owner, creating a unique opportunity to build equity, stabilize expenses, and gain long-term control over the operating environment. This shift from leasing to owning is not just a financial move—it is a strategic transformation that can significantly impact the trajectory of a business and the personal wealth of its owner.

To fully understand the importance of owner-occupied SBA mortgage financing, it is essential to begin with the definition of what qualifies as "owner-occupied" under SBA guidelines. In general, the SBA requires that a business occupy at least 51% of an existing commercial property. For new construction projects, this requirement increases to 60%. This occupancy requirement ensures that the primary purpose of the loan is to support the operating business rather than to serve as a passive investment. This distinction is critical because it is what allows SBA loans to offer more favorable terms compared to traditional commercial real estate loans. By aligning the financing with the operational needs of a business, the SBA reduces risk for lenders and increases accessibility for borrowers.

One of the key benefits of SBA owner-occupied financing is the ability to enter commercial real estate ownership with a relatively low down payment. Traditional commercial loans often require 20% to 30% down, which can be a significant barrier for many small business owners. In contrast, SBA loans—particularly the SBA 7(a) and SBA 504 programs—can allow down payments as low as 10%. This lower equity requirement makes it possible for business owners to preserve cash for operations, marketing, and growth while still acquiring a valuable asset. This balance between ownership and liquidity is one of the defining advantages of SBA financing.

Another defining characteristic of SBA owner-occupied loans is the extended loan term. While many conventional commercial loans have terms of 5 to 10 years with shorter amortization periods, SBA loans can offer terms of up to 25 years for real estate. This extended term results in lower monthly payments, which improves cash flow and reduces financial pressure on the business. For many business owners, this difference in payment structure can mean the difference between a manageable investment and an overwhelming financial burden. Lower payments provide breathing room, allowing the business to grow and adapt without being constrained by high fixed costs.

In addition to favorable down payment and term structures, SBA owner-occupied financing often provides more flexible underwriting criteria. Traditional lenders may place heavy emphasis on historical financial performance and strict ratios, while SBA programs take a more holistic view of the borrower. This includes considering the strength of the business model, the experience of the owner, and the overall viability of the project. This flexibility opens the door for business owners who may not meet conventional lending standards but still have strong potential for success.

A critical component of understanding owner-occupied SBA financing is recognizing the dual role of the borrower. In most cases, the business entity will be the operating company, while a separate entity—often a real estate holding company—will own the property. The operating business then leases the space from the real estate entity. This structure provides several advantages, including liability protection and potential tax benefits. It also allows the business owner to separate the operational risks of the business from the ownership of the real estate, creating a more secure financial foundation.

The relationship between the operating company and the property-owning entity must be structured carefully to meet SBA requirements. The lease agreement between the two entities must reflect fair market terms and must be consistent with the occupancy requirements. Lenders will review this structure closely to ensure compliance and to assess the stability of the arrangement. Understanding how to properly set up these entities and agreements is a crucial step in the financing process and one that can significantly impact the success of the loan application.

Another important aspect of owner-occupied SBA financing is property eligibility. Not all properties qualify for SBA financing, and it is essential to understand the criteria before beginning the search process. Eligible properties typically include office buildings, retail spaces, warehouses, and certain special-use properties such as medical or dental offices. The property must be suitable for the borrower's business operations and must meet appraisal and environmental standards. Properties with excessive deferred maintenance or environmental concerns may face additional scrutiny or may be deemed ineligible.

Location also plays a significant role in the evaluation of a property. Lenders will consider factors such as market demand, property value trends, and the overall economic conditions of the area. A well-located property with strong fundamentals can enhance the strength of the loan application, while a property in a declining or unstable market may present additional challenges. Understanding how lenders assess location can help borrowers make more informed decisions when selecting a property.

As business owners explore the transition from leasing to owning, it is important to compare the long-term financial implications of each option. Leasing may offer flexibility and lower upfront costs, but it does not provide any equity or long-term ownership benefits. Over time, rent payments can increase, and the lack of control over the property can create operational challenges. Ownership, on the other hand, provides stability, equity growth, and the potential for appreciation. While it requires a greater initial commitment, the long-term benefits often outweigh the costs.

Cash flow is another critical consideration in owner-occupied financing. While SBA loans are designed to provide manageable payments, it is still essential for the business to generate sufficient income to cover the debt service. Lenders will evaluate the debt service coverage ratio (DSCR) to ensure that the business can comfortably meet its obligations. A strong DSCR indicates that the business has enough income to support the loan, while a weak DSCR may signal potential risk. Understanding how to calculate and improve this ratio is an important part of preparing for financing.

Risk management is also a key component of owner-occupied property ownership. While ownership provides many benefits, it also comes with responsibilities, including property maintenance, insurance, and potential market fluctuations. Business owners must be prepared to manage these risks and to plan for unexpected expenses. Having adequate reserves and a clear financial strategy can help mitigate these risks and ensure long-term success.

As you progress through this book, you will gain a deeper understanding of how to navigate these complexities and how to leverage SBA financing to achieve your goals. Owner-occupied commercial real estate is not just a financial transaction—it is a strategic decision that can redefine your business and your financial future. By understanding the principles outlined in this chapter, you are taking the first step toward making that transformation.

Real-Life Math Example: Transitioning from Leasing to Owning with an SBA Loan

To fully understand the power of owner-occupied SBA mortgage financing, let's walk through a detailed real-life example that illustrates how the numbers work and how this strategy can impact a business owner's financial position over time. Consider a business owner named Maria who operates a growing dental practice. Maria currently leases a 3,000-square-foot office space for $6,000 per month, with her lease increasing by 3% annually. She has been in business for several years, has stable income, and is now considering purchasing a property for her practice.

Maria identifies a suitable commercial property priced at $900,000. The property meets SBA owner-occupied requirements, and she plans to occupy 100% of the space. She applies for an SBA 504 loan, which allows her to purchase the property with a 10% down payment. This means she needs to invest $90,000 upfront. The remaining $810,000 is financed through a combination of a bank loan and a CDC (Certified Development Company) loan.

The SBA 504 structure typically includes 50% bank financing, 40% CDC financing, and 10% borrower equity. In Maria's case, the bank finances $450,000, and the CDC finances $360,000. The bank portion has an interest rate of 6.5% with a 25-year amortization, while the CDC portion has a fixed rate of 5.5% for 25 years. When combined, Maria's total monthly mortgage payment is approximately $5,500. At first glance, Maria's mortgage payment of $5,500 is already lower than her current rent of $6,000. This immediately improves her monthly cash flow by $500. However, the true advantage becomes clear when we project these numbers over time. If Maria continues leasing, her rent will increase annually. After five years, her rent would rise to approximately $6,950 per month. Over ten years, it could exceed $8,000 per month. In contrast, her SBA loan payment remains relatively stable, providing predictability and protection against rising costs.

Over a 10-year period, Maria would pay approximately $720,000 in rent if she continues leasing, assuming modest increases. This money provides no equity and no ownership. On the other hand, if she purchases the property, a significant portion of her mortgage payments goes toward principal reduction. After 10 years, she may have paid down approximately $200,000 in principal, increasing her equity in the property.

In addition to principal reduction, Maria benefits from property appreciation. If the property appreciates at an average rate of 3% per year, its value would increase from $900,000 to approximately $1.21 million over 10 years. This represents a gain of over $300,000 in value. Combined with her principal reduction, Maria's total equity could exceed $500,000 after a decade. Another important factor to consider is tax savings. Maria may be able to deduct mortgage interest and depreciation, which can reduce her taxable income. While the exact savings depend on her financial situation, these deductions can significantly lower the effective cost of ownership. This further enhances the financial advantage of purchasing the property.

Now consider the long-term impact. After 25 years, Maria's loan is fully paid off. She owns the property outright, eliminating her monthly mortgage payment entirely. At this point, her business operates from a fully owned asset, dramatically reducing overhead costs. If she chooses to retire or sell her practice, the property can be sold separately or included as part of the transaction, potentially increasing the overall value of the deal.

This example highlights the transformative power of owner-occupied SBA financing. By shifting from leasing to owning, Maria not only reduces her monthly expenses but also builds significant long-term wealth. The combination of lower payments, equity growth, appreciation, and tax advantages creates a compelling financial case for ownership.

Understanding these numbers is essential for any business owner considering this transition. While every situation is unique, the underlying principles remain the same. SBA owner-occupied financing provides a pathway to ownership that is both accessible and financially advantageous. By analyzing your current expenses, evaluating potential properties, and structuring your loan effectively, you can make informed decisions that support your business and your financial future.

Chapter 2

SBA Loan Programs for Owner-Occupied Commercial Properties

Understanding the different SBA loan programs available for owner-occupied commercial real estate is essential for any business owner who wants to make a smart, strategic move into property ownership. While many borrowers simply hear "SBA loan" and assume it is a single product, the reality is that there are multiple SBA financing options, each with its own structure, advantages, and ideal use cases. The two primary programs used for owner-occupied commercial real estate are the SBA 7(a) loan and the SBA 504 loan. Each serves a specific purpose, and choosing the right one can significantly impact your cash flow, long-term equity, and overall financial strategy.

The SBA 7(a) loan is the most flexible and widely used SBA financing program. It is designed to support a broad range of business needs, including real estate acquisition, working capital, equipment purchases, and even refinancing existing debt. This flexibility makes the 7(a) loan particularly attractive for business owners who need more than just property financing. For example, if a borrower wants to purchase a building and also fund renovations, cover closing costs, and maintain cash reserves, the 7(a) program can often bundle these needs into a single loan. This eliminates the need for multiple financing sources and simplifies the overall transaction.

One of the defining characteristics of the SBA 7(a) loan is that it is provided entirely by a lender, with the SBA guaranteeing a portion of the loan to reduce the lender's risk. This guarantee allows lenders to offer more favorable terms than they might otherwise provide. Typical features of a 7(a) loan include down payments starting at around 10%, amortization periods of up to 25 years for real estate, and variable or fixed interest rate options. Because of its flexibility, the 7(a) loan is often the go-to choice for smaller projects or situations where the borrower needs additional funds beyond just the property purchase.

In contrast, the SBA 504 loan is specifically designed for fixed asset purchases, particularly commercial real estate and large equipment. It is structured differently from the 7(a) loan and involves three parties: a bank, a Certified Development Company (CDC), and the borrower. The typical structure includes 50% financing from a bank, 40% from the CDC (backed by the SBA), and 10% from the borrower. This structure is one of the most powerful features of the 504 program because it allows borrowers to secure long-term, fixed-rate financing on a significant portion of the loan. The SBA 504 loan is especially attractive for business owners who prioritize stability and long-term planning. The CDC portion of the loan is typically fixed for 20 or 25 years, providing predictable payments and protection against interest rate increases. This makes it an ideal option for businesses that want to lock in their occupancy costs and avoid the uncertainty of rising rates. While the bank portion may have a variable rate, the overall blended rate is often competitive and manageable.

Another key difference between the 7(a) and 504 programs is how funds can be used. The 504 loan is more restrictive and is primarily limited to real estate and equipment. It cannot be used for working capital or inventory. However, this limitation is also what allows the program to offer such favorable long-term terms. By focusing on fixed assets, the SBA can structure the loan in a way that aligns with the long-term nature of real estate ownership.

Choosing between the SBA 7(a) and 504 loan programs requires a clear understanding of your business goals and financial needs. If you need maximum flexibility and additional funds for business operations, the 7(a) loan may be the better option. If your primary goal is to acquire real estate with stable, long-term financing and minimal down payment, the 504 loan may be the ideal choice. In some cases, borrowers may even use a combination of financing strategies to achieve their objectives. Another important consideration is the size and scope of the project. SBA 7(a) loans have a maximum loan amount of $5 million, which can limit their use for larger commercial real estate transactions. SBA 504 loans, on the other hand, can support larger projects through the CDC portion, especially when certain public policy goals are met, such as job creation or energy efficiency improvements. Understanding these limits can help you determine which program aligns with your investment strategy.

Interest rates also play a critical role in the decision-making process. SBA 7(a) loans often have variable rates tied to the prime rate, which means payments can fluctuate over time. While this can be beneficial in a low-rate environment, it introduces uncertainty in the long term. SBA 504 loans offer fixed rates on the CDC portion, providing greater predictability. This difference can have a significant impact on long-term financial planning, especially for businesses operating on tight margins.

The approval process for SBA loans also varies between programs. While both require detailed documentation, including financial statements, tax returns, and business plans, the 504 loan involves coordination between multiple parties, which can extend the timeline. However, this additional complexity is often offset by the benefits of long-term fixed financing. Borrowers who are prepared and organized can navigate this process efficiently and position themselves for success.

It is also important to understand how lenders evaluate SBA loan applications. Regardless of the program, lenders will assess the borrower's creditworthiness, business performance, and ability to repay the loan. They will look at key metrics such as debt service coverage ratio, cash flow stability, and industry risk. By understanding these criteria, borrowers can proactively strengthen their applications and increase their chances of approval.

Another strategic advantage of SBA loan programs is their ability to support business growth beyond the initial property purchase. For example, a business owner who acquires a property using an SBA loan may later leverage that asset to secure additional financing for expansion, equipment upgrades, or new locations. This creates a compounding effect, where one strategic decision leads to multiple growth opportunities over time.

As you move forward in your journey, it is essential to view SBA financing not just as a loan, but as a long-term strategic tool. The program you choose, the structure you implement, and the decisions you make during the process will all have lasting implications for your business. By taking the time to understand the nuances of each program, you position yourself to make informed decisions that align with your goals.

This chapter provides the foundation for understanding how SBA loan programs work in the context of owner-occupied commercial real estate. In the chapters that follow, you will build on this knowledge and learn how to apply it in real-world scenarios, structure your deals effectively, and maximize the benefits of SBA financing.

Real-Life Math Example: Comparing SBA 7(a) vs SBA 504 for an Owner-Occupied Purchase

Let's consider a real-world scenario to illustrate how the SBA 7(a) and SBA 504 loan programs compare when financing an owner-occupied commercial property. Imagine a business owner named David who operates a successful auto repair shop. David is currently leasing his space for $7,500 per month and wants to purchase a property valued at $1,200,000 to establish a permanent location for his business.

First, let's analyze the SBA 7(a) option. David qualifies for a

10% down payment, which means he needs to invest $120,000 upfront. The remaining $1,080,000 is financed through a single loan. Assuming an interest rate of 7.5% with a 25-year amortization, David's monthly payment would be approximately $8,000. This is slightly higher than his current rent, but it includes both principal and interest, meaning he is building equity with each payment.

Over the first five years, David would pay approximately $480,000 in total payments. Of this amount, roughly $100,000 would go toward principal reduction, while the rest covers interest. This means that after five years, David has already built significant equity in the property. If the property appreciates at 3% annually, its value would increase to approximately $1,390,000, adding nearly $190,000 in appreciation. Combined with his principal reduction, David's total equity after five years could exceed $290,000.

Now let's compare this with the SBA 504 option. With the same property value of $1,200,000, David still invests $120,000 as a 10% down payment. The bank finances $600,000 at 6.5%, and the CDC finances $480,000 at 5.5%. The combined monthly payment is approximately $7,200, which is actually lower than his current rent. This immediate cash flow improvement makes the 504 loan particularly attractive.

Over five years, David would pay approximately $432,000 in total payments under the 504 structure. Because of the lower interest rates and structured financing, a larger portion of these payments goes toward principal reduction. After five years, he may have reduced the principal by approximately $120,000. When combined with the same appreciation scenario, his total equity could exceed $310,000.

Now consider the long-term impact over 25 years. With the SBA 7(a) loan, David's payments may fluctuate if the interest rate is variable, potentially increasing his total cost. With the SBA 504 loan, the CDC portion remains fixed, providing stability and predictability. This can result in significant savings over the life of the loan, especially in a rising interest rate environment.

Let's also compare this to continuing to lease. If David continues paying $7,500 per month with a 3% annual increase, he would pay approximately $2.6 million in rent over 25 years. This money provides no equity and no ownership. In contrast, both SBA loan options allow him to own a valuable asset that may be worth over $2 million by the end of the term, depending on market conditions.

This example clearly demonstrates the power of SBA loan programs for owner-occupied commercial real estate. While both the 7(a) and 504 loans provide a pathway to ownership, the differences in structure, rates, and long-term impact can significantly influence the outcome. By understanding these differences and analyzing the numbers, business owners can make informed decisions that align with their financial goals and set the foundation for long-term success.

Chapter 3

Structuring Owner-Occupied SBA Mortgage Deals for Maximum Approval

Structuring an owner-occupied SBA mortgage deal is one of the most critical aspects of successfully obtaining financing and building a long-term wealth strategy through commercial real estate. While many borrowers focus primarily on credit scores or income, the truth is that deal structure often plays an even more important role in whether a loan is approved or denied. A well-structured deal can compensate for minor weaknesses in a borrower's profile, while a poorly structured deal can lead to rejection even when the borrower appears strong on paper. Understanding how to properly structure your SBA mortgage transaction is essential if you want to maximize approval chances, secure favorable terms, and create a foundation for long-term financial growth.

At the core of deal structuring is the relationship between the borrower, the operating business, and the property itself. In most owner-occupied SBA transactions, the borrower will create or use two entities: an operating company that runs the business and a separate real estate holding company that owns the property. This structure is widely used because it provides both legal and financial advantages. The operating company signs a lease and pays rent to the real estate entity, while the real estate entity holds the mortgage. This separation helps protect the property from business liabilities and allows for more flexibility in long-term planning, including potential sale or lease strategies.

However, simply creating two entities is not enough. The relationship between them must be structured properly to meet SBA requirements. The SBA requires that the operating company and the real estate holding company have common ownership, typically at least 51%. The lease agreement between the two must also reflect fair market terms, even though both entities are controlled by the same owner. Lenders will review this structure carefully to ensure compliance and to confirm that the transaction is legitimate and sustainable. Any inconsistencies or red flags in this structure can delay or jeopardize approval.

Another key component of deal structuring is the down payment. While SBA loans allow for relatively low down payments—often as low as 10%—how that down payment is sourced and documented is critical. Lenders need to verify that the funds are legitimate, seasoned, and not borrowed in a way that increases risk. Acceptable sources include personal savings, business reserves, or in some cases, gifted funds. Some borrowers may also use seller contributions or partial financing structures, but these must be carefully structured to meet SBA guidelines. Understanding how to properly present and document your equity injection can significantly strengthen your application.

Cash flow is another major factor in deal structuring. Lenders will evaluate the business's ability to support the new mortgage payment using the debt service coverage ratio (DSCR). A DSCR of 1.25 or higher is typically preferred, meaning the business generates at least 25% more income than required to cover its debt obligations. Structuring your deal to achieve a strong DSCR may involve adjusting the loan amount, negotiating the purchase price, or improving your financial presentation. For example, adding back certain expenses or demonstrating consistent revenue trends can improve your DSCR and increase your chances of approval.

The purchase price itself is also a critical element of deal structuring. While it may be tempting to focus solely on securing the property, overpaying can create challenges during the appraisal process. SBA lenders rely heavily on appraisals to determine the value of the property, and if the appraised value comes in lower than the purchase price, the borrower may need to increase their down payment or renegotiate the deal. Structuring your offer based on realistic market values and comparable sales can help avoid these issues and ensure a smoother transaction.

Another strategic element is the use of seller concessions and credits. In some cases, the seller may agree to cover a portion of the closing costs or provide credits for repairs or improvements. These concessions can reduce the borrower's upfront cash requirements and improve overall deal feasibility. However, they must be structured within SBA guidelines to ensure compliance. Lenders will review these arrangements to confirm that they do not artificially inflate the purchase price or create hidden risks.

Loan term and interest rate selection also play a significant role in structuring your deal. Choosing between fixed and variable rates, as well as selecting the appropriate loan program (such as SBA 7(a) or 504), can impact your monthly payment, cash flow, and long-term financial stability. Structuring your loan to align with your business's cash flow and growth projections is essential. For example, a longer amortization period can reduce monthly payments, improving DSCR and increasing approval likelihood.

Another often overlooked aspect of deal structuring is the borrower's experience and industry background. SBA lenders place significant value on the borrower's ability to successfully operate the business. If the borrower has prior experience in the same or a related industry, it strengthens the application. If not, the deal may need to be structured with additional support, such as a qualified management team or a detailed business plan. Demonstrating competence and preparedness can make a substantial difference in how lenders perceive risk.

Collateral is another important consideration. While the property itself serves as the primary collateral, lenders may also require additional collateral, especially if there is a shortfall in value. This could include personal real estate or other assets. Structuring your deal to minimize collateral requirements—by ensuring a strong appraisal and adequate down payment—can help protect your personal assets and simplify the transaction.

Timing also plays a critical role in deal structuring. The process of securing an SBA loan can take several weeks or even months, depending on the complexity of the transaction. Aligning your purchase agreement, due diligence period, and financing timeline is essential to avoid delays or contract issues. Working with experienced professionals, including brokers, lenders, and attorneys, can help ensure that all elements of the deal are coordinated effectively.

One of the most powerful strategies in SBA deal structuring is thinking several steps ahead. Instead of focusing solely on the current transaction, consider how this property will fit into your long-term plans. Will it support future expansion? Can it generate additional income through leasing excess space? Will it be part of your exit strategy? Structuring your deal with these considerations in mind can enhance its value and create additional opportunities down the line.

Risk mitigation is also a key component of successful deal structuring. This includes conducting thorough due diligence on the property, understanding market conditions, and preparing for potential challenges. Environmental reports, property inspections, and financial audits are all part of this process. Identifying and addressing potential issues early can prevent costly surprises and strengthen your position with lenders.

Ultimately, structuring an owner-occupied SBA mortgage deal is both an art and a science. It requires a deep understanding of financial principles, lender expectations, and strategic planning. By mastering these elements, you can position yourself as a strong borrower, secure favorable financing, and build a solid foundation for long-term success. This chapter provides the framework you need to approach deal structuring with confidence and clarity.

Real-Life Math Example: Structuring a Deal to Improve Approval and Cash Flow

Let's walk through a detailed real-life scenario to understand how proper deal structuring can impact loan approval and financial outcomes. Consider a business owner named Kevin who operates a growing logistics company. Kevin currently leases a warehouse for $8,500 per month and wants to purchase a larger facility to support his expansion. He identifies a property priced at $1,500,000.

Initially, Kevin plans to proceed with a straightforward SBA 7(a) loan with a 10% down payment of $150,000. The remaining $1,350,000 would be financed at an interest rate of 7.5% over 25 years. This results in a monthly payment of approximately $10,000. While Kevin's business generates strong revenue, his current net operating income supports a DSCR of only 1.15 with this payment, which is below the preferred threshold of 1.25. This creates a potential challenge for loan approval.

To improve the structure, Kevin and his advisor explore several adjustments. First, they negotiate the purchase price down to $1,400,000 based on comparable sales and minor property issues identified during inspection. This reduces the loan amount to $1,260,000 after a 10% down payment of $140,000. The new monthly payment drops to approximately

$9,300. Next, Kevin decides to increase his down payment slightly to $200,000 by using additional business reserves. This further reduces the loan amount to $1,200,000, bringing the monthly payment down to approximately $8,900. This adjustment alone significantly improves the DSCR.

Additionally, Kevin identifies an opportunity to lease out a small unused portion of the warehouse to another business for $1,500 per month. This additional income is included in the underwriting, further strengthening his DSCR. With these combined adjustments, Kevin's DSCR increases to approximately 1.35, well above the lender's requirement.

Now let's analyze the long-term impact. With the improved structure, Kevin's monthly payment is only slightly higher than his current rent, but he is now building equity with each payment. Over the first 10 years, he may pay down approximately $250,000 in principal. If the property appreciates at 3% annually, its value could increase to over $2 million, adding significant equity.

If Kevin had proceeded with the original structure, he might have faced a loan denial or been forced to accept less favorable terms. By strategically adjusting the purchase price, down payment, and income structure, he not only secured approval but also created a more sustainable financial position. This example highlights the importance of proactive deal structuring. Small adjustments can have a significant impact on approval, cash flow, and long-term wealth. By understanding the key variables and how they interact, business owners can take control of the process and position themselves for success.

Chapter 4

Qualifying for an Owner-Occupied SBA Mortgage Loan

Qualifying for an owner-occupied SBA mortgage loan is a process that goes far beyond simply having good credit or steady income. It is a comprehensive evaluation of your financial strength, business stability, experience, and ability to manage risk over the long term. SBA lenders are not just approving a loan—they are making a decision about whether your business can sustain and grow while supporting a significant financial obligation. Understanding how to position yourself for approval is one of the most important steps in transitioning from leasing to owning your commercial property.

At the foundation of SBA loan qualification is your credit profile. While SBA loans are more flexible than traditional commercial loans, lenders still expect borrowers to demonstrate responsible credit behavior. This typically means a personal credit score in the mid-600s or higher, although stronger scores will always improve your chances. Beyond the score itself, lenders look at your credit history, including payment patterns, outstanding debts, and any past issues such as collections or bankruptcies. A clean and consistent credit history signals reliability and reduces perceived risk.

Equally important is your business's financial performance. Lenders will carefully review your business tax returns, profit and loss statements, and balance sheets, typically for the past two to three years. They are looking for consistent revenue, stable or growing profits, and a clear ability to generate cash flow. This cash flow is what ultimately supports your loan payments, so it must be sufficient and predictable. If your business has experienced fluctuations, you must be prepared to explain them and demonstrate how stability has been achieved or will be achieved moving forward.

One of the most critical metrics in SBA loan qualification is the debt service coverage ratio (DSCR). This ratio measures your business's ability to cover its debt obligations, including the new mortgage. A DSCR of 1.25 is generally considered the minimum acceptable level, meaning your business generates 25% more income than needed to cover the debt. A higher DSCR provides a stronger cushion and increases lender confidence. If your DSCR is borderline, you may need to adjust your deal structure, reduce your loan amount, or improve your financial presentation to meet lender requirements.

Your personal financial strength also plays a significant role in the qualification process. SBA loans typically require a personal guarantee, which means you are personally responsible for the loan if the business cannot repay it. Lenders will review your personal financial statement, including assets, liabilities, and net worth. They want to see that you have financial stability and the ability to support the loan if needed. This includes having sufficient liquidity, such as savings or other accessible funds, to cover unexpected expenses or temporary downturns in business performance.

Experience and industry knowledge are often overlooked but highly important factors in SBA loan approval. Lenders want to know that you have the expertise to successfully operate your business in the property you are financing. If you have several years of experience in your industry, it strengthens your application significantly. If you are entering a new industry, you may need to provide additional support, such as a detailed business plan, experienced management team, or training certifications, to demonstrate your capability.

Another key component of qualification is the equity injection, or down payment. While SBA loans allow for lower down payments compared to conventional loans, you are still required to invest in the project. This investment shows commitment and reduces the lender's risk. The source of these funds must be documented and verified. Lenders prefer funds that are seasoned, meaning they have been in your account for a period of time, typically at least 60 days. Large unexplained deposits can raise concerns and may require additional documentation.

Collateral is also part of the qualification process. While the property being financed serves as the primary collateral, lenders may require additional collateral if there is a shortfall in value or if the loan is considered higher risk. This could include personal real estate or other assets. The goal for the lender is to ensure that there is sufficient security for the loan. Structuring your deal to minimize collateral requirements—such as by ensuring a strong appraisal and adequate down payment—can simplify the process and protect your personal assets.

The property itself must also meet SBA eligibility requirements. It must be suitable for your business operations and meet the owner-occupancy criteria. Additionally, the property must pass appraisal and environmental reviews. Lenders will order a professional appraisal to determine the market value of the property and ensure that it supports the loan amount. Environmental reports are also required to identify any potential hazards or contamination that could pose risks. These evaluations are critical and can impact both approval and timing.

Another important factor is your business's legal and organizational structure. Lenders will review your business formation documents, operating agreements, and ownership structure to ensure compliance with SBA requirements. The ownership of the operating company and the real estate holding company must align with SBA guidelines, typically requiring at least 51% common ownership. Proper documentation and organization are essential to avoid delays and ensure a smooth approval process.

Liquidity and reserves are also key considerations. Lenders want to see that you have enough cash reserves to handle unexpected challenges after closing. This may include covering several months of mortgage payments, operating expenses, or repairs. Having strong reserves not only improves your chances of approval but also provides peace of mind as you transition into property ownership.

The application process itself requires careful preparation and attention to detail. You will need to provide a comprehensive package of documents, including financial statements, tax returns, business plans, and personal information. Missing or incomplete documentation can delay the process and create frustration. Working with experienced professionals, such as a mortgage broker or SBA lender, can help you navigate this process efficiently and avoid common pitfalls.

Timing is another important aspect of qualification. Preparing for an SBA loan should begin well before you identify a property. This allows you to address any issues, strengthen your financial profile, and position yourself as a strong borrower. By the time you are ready to make an offer, you should have a clear understanding of your qualifications and be prepared to move quickly.

Ultimately, qualifying for an owner-occupied SBA mortgage loan is about demonstrating strength, stability, and readiness. It is about showing lenders that you have a viable business, a solid financial foundation, and a clear plan for success. By understanding the qualification criteria and preparing accordingly, you can significantly increase your chances of approval and move forward with confidence.

Real-Life Math Example: Qualifying Based on Income, DSCR, and Financial Strength

Let's walk through a detailed real-life scenario to understand how qualification works from a financial perspective. Consider a business owner named Lisa who operates a successful physical therapy clinic. Lisa is currently leasing her space for

$5,500 per month and wants to purchase a property valued at $950,000 to expand her operations.

Lisa applies for an SBA loan with a 10% down payment of $95,000. The remaining $855,000 is financed at an interest rate of 7% over 25 years. This results in a monthly mortgage payment of approximately $6,050. At first glance, this is slightly higher than her current rent, but the key question is whether her business income can support this payment.

Lisa's business generates an annual net operating income of $120,000. To calculate her DSCR, we divide her annual income by her annual debt service. Her annual mortgage payments total approximately $72,600 ($6,050 multiplied by 12 months). Dividing $120,000 by $72,600 gives a DSCR of approximately 1.65. This is well above the minimum requirement of 1.25, indicating strong ability to cover the loan.

However, lenders also consider other obligations. Lisa has an existing business loan with monthly payments of $1,000, or $12,000 annually. Adding this to her mortgage payments brings her total annual debt service to $84,600. Recalculating her DSCR, we divide $120,000 by $84,600, resulting in a DSCR of approximately 1.42. This is still strong and within acceptable limits.

Now let's consider her personal financial position. Lisa has

$150,000 in savings, which she uses to cover her $95,000 down payment and still retains $55,000 in reserves. This demonstrates strong liquidity and provides a safety net for unexpected expenses. Her personal credit score is 720, and she has no significant negative credit history. These factors further strengthen her application.

Next, we evaluate the long-term impact. Over the first 10 years, Lisa will pay approximately $726,000 in total mortgage payments. Of this amount, a significant portion goes toward principal reduction. She may build approximately $200,000 in equity during this period. If the property appreciates at 3% annually, its value could increase to approximately $1.28 million, adding over $300,000 in value.

Now compare this to leasing. If Lisa continues paying $5,500 per month with a 3% annual increase, she would pay approximately $760,000 in rent over 10 years. This provides no equity and no ownership. In contrast, by purchasing the property, she not only covers her occupancy costs but also builds substantial wealth.

This example illustrates how lenders evaluate qualification using real numbers. By analyzing income, debt obligations, and financial strength, they determine whether the borrower can sustain the loan. For Lisa, strong income, manageable debt, and solid reserves make her an ideal candidate for SBA financing.

Understanding these calculations allows you to prepare effectively and position yourself for approval. By improving your income, managing your debts, and maintaining strong financial reserves, you can meet lender requirements and take the next step toward owning your business property.

Chapter 5

Finding and Evaluating the Right Owner-Occupied Commercial Property

Finding the right owner-occupied commercial property is one of the most important decisions a business owner will make when transitioning from leasing to ownership. While financing, qualification, and deal structure are all critical components of the process, the property itself ultimately determines whether the investment will support long-term success or create ongoing challenges. The right property can enhance operations, improve efficiency, increase revenue potential, and build equity over time. The wrong property can strain cash flow, limit growth, and introduce unnecessary risks. Understanding how to properly identify and evaluate commercial real estate is essential to making a smart, strategic decision.

The process begins with clarity around your business needs. Before searching for a property, you must define how the space will be used and what requirements are essential for your operations. This includes factors such as square footage, layout, parking availability, accessibility, zoning, and future expansion potential. Many business owners make the mistake of focusing solely on what they need today, without considering how their business may grow over the next five to ten years. An ideal property should not only meet current needs but also provide flexibility for future expansion, additional services, or increased capacity.

Location is one of the most critical factors in evaluating a commercial property. The old saying "location, location, location" holds true because the success of many businesses is directly tied to their physical presence. For retail and service-based businesses, visibility, foot traffic, and proximity to target customers are essential. For industrial or logistics businesses, access to major roads, highways, and transportation hubs may be more important. Lenders also evaluate location as part of their risk assessment, so choosing a strong, stable market can improve both your business performance and your financing prospects.

Market analysis plays a key role in property evaluation. Understanding the local real estate market helps you determine whether a property is priced appropriately and whether it has the potential for appreciation. This involves analyzing comparable sales, rental rates, vacancy rates, and economic trends in the area. A property that is priced below market value may present an opportunity, while an overpriced property could lead to appraisal issues and financing challenges. Taking the time to study the market ensures that you are making an informed decision rather than relying on assumptions.

Another important consideration is the condition of the property. A thorough inspection is essential to identify any structural, mechanical, or environmental issues that could impact your investment. This includes evaluating the roof, HVAC systems, plumbing, electrical systems, and overall structural integrity. Deferred maintenance or hidden problems can result in significant repair costs after closing, which can strain your finances and disrupt your operations. Identifying these issues early allows you to negotiate repairs, request credits, or reconsider the purchase if necessary.

Zoning and compliance are also critical factors in property evaluation. The property must be zoned appropriately for your business operations, and any planned changes or expansions must comply with local regulations. Failure to verify zoning can lead to costly delays or even prevent you from operating your business as intended. Additionally, SBA lenders require that properties meet certain eligibility criteria, so ensuring compliance with both local regulations and SBA guidelines is essential.

Another key aspect of evaluating a property is its income potential. Even though the property is owner-occupied, there may be opportunities to generate additional income by leasing unused space to other tenants. This can improve your cash flow and strengthen your loan application by increasing your DSCR. When evaluating a property, consider whether there is excess space that could be rented out and whether the local market supports such leasing opportunities. This added income can significantly enhance the overall value of the investment.

Appraisal value is another critical component of the evaluation process. Lenders rely on professional appraisals to determine the fair market value of the property. If the appraisal comes in lower than the purchase price, it can create challenges in securing financing. Understanding how appraisals work and ensuring that your purchase price aligns with market value can help avoid these issues. Working with experienced real estate professionals and reviewing comparable sales can provide valuable insights into pricing.

Environmental considerations are also part of the evaluation process. SBA loans typically require environmental assessments to identify potential hazards such as contamination or hazardous materials. These issues can pose significant risks and may require remediation before financing can be approved. Understanding the environmental status of a property is essential to avoiding unexpected costs and ensuring compliance with lender requirements.

Future growth potential is another important factor to consider. A property that meets your needs today but limits your ability to expand may not be the best long-term investment. Consider whether the property allows for expansion, renovation, or additional development. Properties with flexible layouts or additional land may provide opportunities for future growth, increasing their value and utility over time.

Another strategic consideration is the potential for appreciation. While no investment is guaranteed, properties in strong markets with growing demand are more likely to increase in value over time. Factors such as population growth, economic development, and infrastructure improvements can all contribute to appreciation. Evaluating these trends can help you identify properties with strong long-term potential.

Financing considerations should also be integrated into your property evaluation. Not all properties qualify for SBA financing, and certain characteristics—such as excessive vacancy, specialized use, or environmental concerns—can complicate the approval process. Understanding lender requirements and evaluating properties through that lens can save time and prevent disappointment later in the process.

Negotiation is another critical aspect of acquiring the right property. Once you identify a suitable property, the ability to negotiate effectively can impact both your upfront costs and long-term financial performance. This includes negotiating the purchase price, repair credits, closing costs, and other terms. A well-negotiated deal can improve your cash flow, reduce your risk, and increase your overall return on investment.

Ultimately, finding and evaluating the right owner-occupied commercial property requires a combination of analysis, strategy, and foresight. It is not just about finding a space—it is about identifying an asset that supports your business, aligns with your financial goals, and provides long-term value. By approaching this process with a clear framework and a disciplined mindset, you can make decisions that position you for success.

Real-Life Math Example: Evaluating Property Value, Cash Flow, and Long-Term Return

Let's walk through a detailed real-life example to illustrate how to evaluate a commercial property from both a financial and strategic perspective. Consider a business owner named Anthony who operates a growing fitness center. Anthony is currently leasing a space for $9,000 per month and is looking to purchase a property to establish a permanent location.

Anthony identifies two potential properties. Property A is priced at $1,300,000 and requires minimal renovations. Property B is priced at $1,150,000 but requires $150,000 in improvements. At first glance, both properties have a similar total investment of approximately $1,300,000, but their financial implications differ significantly.

For Property A, Anthony would need a 10% down payment of $130,000, with a loan amount of $1,170,000. Assuming an interest rate of 7% over 25 years, his monthly payment would be approximately $8,300. This is slightly lower than his current rent, providing immediate cash flow improvement.

For Property B, Anthony would need a 10% down payment of $115,000 plus $150,000 in renovation costs, for a total upfront investment of $265,000. The loan amount would be $1,035,000, resulting in a monthly payment of approximately $7,300. While the monthly payment is lower, the higher upfront investment reduces his available cash reserves.

Now let's evaluate long-term equity and appreciation. Assuming both properties appreciate at 3% annually, Property A would increase in value from $1,300,000 to approximately $1,750,000 over 10 years. Property B, starting at a lower purchase price but with improvements, may also reach a similar value, but the timing and risk of renovations must be considered.

Over 10 years, Anthony would pay approximately $996,000 in mortgage payments for Property A, with a significant portion going toward principal reduction. He may build approximately $250,000 in equity during this period. For Property B, his total payments would be lower, and he may build slightly more equity due to the smaller loan amount, but this must be weighed against the higher upfront investment and renovation risk.

Now compare this to leasing. If Anthony continues paying $9,000 per month with a 3% annual increase, he would pay approximately $1.25 million in rent over 10 years. This provides no equity and no ownership. In contrast, both property options allow him to build substantial equity while controlling his operating environment.

Additionally, consider the potential for additional income. Property A includes an extra 1,000 square feet that Anthony can lease to another business for $2,000 per month. This reduces his effective mortgage cost to approximately $6,300 per month, significantly improving cash flow. Property B does not offer this opportunity, which impacts its overall financial performance.

By analyzing these factors—purchase price, renovation costs, monthly payments, appreciation, and income potential—Anthony can make an informed decision. While both properties have similar total costs, Property A offers better cash flow, lower upfront risk, and additional income potential, making it the stronger investment. This example demonstrates the importance of evaluating commercial properties from multiple angles. It is not just about the purchase price—it is about understanding how each factor impacts your cash flow, equity, and long-term financial outcome. By applying this level of analysis, you can identify opportunities that align with your goals and avoid costly mistakes.

Chapter 6

The SBA Loan Application Process Step-by-Step

The SBA loan application process for owner-occupied commercial real estate can seem complex at first, but when broken down into clear steps, it becomes a structured and manageable path to property ownership. Understanding each phase of the process not only reduces stress but also significantly increases your chances of approval. This chapter will walk you through the complete SBA loan journey—from preparation to closing—so you can approach it with confidence, clarity, and control.

The first and most important step in the SBA loan process is preparation. Before you ever submit an application or make an offer on a property, you should assess your financial position, business performance, and readiness for ownership. This includes reviewing your credit, organizing your financial statements, and calculating your debt service coverage ratio (DSCR). Preparation also involves identifying any potential weaknesses—such as inconsistent income or limited reserves—and addressing them in advance. The more prepared you are at the beginning, the smoother the process will be. Once you are prepared, the next step is prequalification. This is an initial evaluation conducted by a lender or broker to determine whether you meet the basic criteria for an SBA loan. During this stage, you will provide high-level information about your business, income, credit, and the type of property you are considering. The lender will use this information to give you an estimate of how much you can borrow, what your terms might look like, and whether there are any potential issues to address. Prequalification is not a formal approval, but it is a critical step in setting expectations and guiding your property search.

After prequalification, the next phase is selecting a lender and structuring your deal. Not all lenders are the same, and choosing the right one can make a significant difference in your experience. Some lenders specialize in SBA loans and have streamlined processes, while others may be less experienced and slower to respond. Working with a knowledgeable lender or broker who understands owner-occupied SBA financing can help you structure your deal effectively and avoid common pitfalls. This includes determining the appropriate loan program, down payment, and overall financing strategy.

Once you have identified a property and structured your deal, the next step is submitting a formal application. This involves providing a comprehensive package of documentation, including business and personal tax returns, financial statements, bank statements, business plans, and legal documents. The goal of this package is to present a complete and accurate picture of your financial position and business operations. Attention to detail is critical at this stage, as missing or inconsistent information can delay the process or raise concerns with the lender.

After your application is submitted, the loan enters the underwriting phase. This is where the lender conducts a detailed analysis of your financials, credit, and the overall transaction. Underwriters evaluate your ability to repay the loan, assess the risk of the deal, and ensure compliance with SBA guidelines. They may request additional information or clarification during this stage, which is known as "conditions." Responding to these requests quickly and thoroughly is essential to keeping the process moving forward.

At the same time, the lender will order third-party reports, including an appraisal, environmental assessment, and sometimes a property condition report. The appraisal determines the market value of the property and ensures that it supports the loan amount. The environmental report identifies any potential hazards or contamination, while the property condition report evaluates the physical state of the building. These reports are critical components of the approval process and can impact both the timeline and the final terms of the loan. Once underwriting is complete and all conditions have been satisfied, the loan moves into the approval stage. At this point, the lender issues a formal loan commitment outlining the terms and conditions of the financing. This document serves as a roadmap for closing and includes details such as the loan amount, interest rate, repayment terms, and any remaining requirements. Reviewing this commitment carefully is important to ensure that it aligns with your expectations and financial goals.

The next phase is closing preparation. During this stage, final documents are prepared, and all remaining conditions must be cleared. This includes verifying your down payment funds, finalizing insurance coverage, and ensuring that all legal documents are in place. You will also work with a title company or attorney to conduct a title search and prepare closing documents. This phase requires coordination between multiple parties, including the lender, borrower, and closing agents.

Closing is the final step in the SBA loan process. At closing, you will sign all necessary documents, transfer funds, and officially take ownership of the property. This is the culmination of the entire process and marks the beginning of your journey as a property owner. After closing, your focus shifts from securing financing to managing your property and leveraging it for business growth. Throughout this process, communication and organization are key. Staying in regular contact with your lender, responding promptly to requests, and keeping your documentation organized can significantly reduce delays and improve your experience. Working with experienced professionals—such as mortgage brokers, real estate agents, and attorneys—can also provide valuable guidance and support.

Another important aspect of the SBA loan process is timing. From application to closing, the process can take anywhere from 45 to 90 days, depending on the complexity of the transaction and the responsiveness of all parties involved. Planning your timeline carefully and setting realistic expectations can help you navigate this process more effectively.

Ultimately, the SBA loan application process is a structured journey that rewards preparation, organization, and strategic thinking. By understanding each step and approaching it with confidence, you can move from being a tenant to a property owner and take a significant step toward building long-term wealth.

Real-Life Math Example: Timeline, Costs, and Cash Flow Through the SBA Loan Process

Let's walk through a detailed real-life example to understand how the SBA loan process impacts costs, timing, and financial outcomes. Consider a business owner named Daniel who operates a manufacturing company. Daniel is currently leasing a facility for $10,000 per month and wants to purchase a property valued at $1,400,000.

Daniel begins with prequalification and determines that he can qualify for an SBA loan with a 10% down payment of $140,000. His loan amount will be $1,260,000 at an interest rate of 7% over 25 years, resulting in a monthly payment of approximately $8,900. This represents an immediate monthly savings of $1,100 compared to his current rent.

Now let's break down the costs involved in the application process. Daniel pays approximately $5,000 for an appraisal, $2,500 for an environmental report, and $3,500 in legal and closing preparation fees. In total, his upfront costs, excluding the down payment, are approximately $11,000. While these costs may seem significant, they are part of securing a long-term asset that will generate equity and stability.

The timeline for Daniel's loan process is approximately 60 days. During this time, he continues to pay rent, totaling

$20,000 over two months. However, once the loan closes, his monthly payments drop to $8,900, resulting in immediate savings.

Over the first year, Daniel pays approximately $106,800 in mortgage payments. Of this amount, a portion goes toward principal reduction, building equity in the property. If we assume that approximately $20,000 goes toward principal in the first year, Daniel is effectively converting a portion of his monthly expense into ownership.

Now let's project this over 10 years. Daniel will pay approximately $1,068,000 in total mortgage payments. During this time, he may reduce the principal by approximately $300,000, depending on the amortization schedule. If the property appreciates at 3% annually, its value could increase from $1,400,000 to approximately $1,880,000, adding $480,000 in value.

In contrast, if Daniel continues leasing, he would pay $10,000 per month with a 3% annual increase. Over 10 years, this would total approximately $1.39 million in rent, with no equity gained. By purchasing the property, Daniel not only reduces his monthly expenses but also builds substantial wealth.

Additionally, consider the impact of timing. By completing the loan process in 60 days, Daniel minimizes his overlap between rent and mortgage payments. If delays had extended the process to 90 days, he would have paid an additional $10,000 in rent, reducing his overall savings. This highlights the importance of efficiency and organization during the application process. This example demonstrates how the SBA loan process affects not only approval but also financial outcomes. By understanding the timeline, costs, and long-term benefits, business owners can approach the process strategically and make informed decisions that support their goals.

Chapter 7

Closing the Deal and Transitioning from Tenant to Owner

Closing on an owner-occupied commercial property through an SBA mortgage loan is one of the most rewarding milestones in a business owner's journey. It represents the culmination of planning, preparation, underwriting, and negotiation. However, while many borrowers focus heavily on getting approved, the closing phase and the transition into ownership are equally critical. This stage determines how smoothly the transaction is finalized, how effectively the property is integrated into your business operations, and how successfully you begin building long-term wealth. Understanding what happens at closing—and what comes immediately after—is essential to maximizing the benefits of ownership.

The closing process begins once your loan has received final approval and all underwriting conditions have been satisfied. At this point, the lender prepares the final loan documents, which outline the terms and obligations of the financing. These documents include the promissory note, deed of trust or mortgage, personal guarantee, and various disclosures. It is important to review these documents carefully, as they define your financial responsibilities for the life of the loan. While many borrowers rely on their lender or attorney to guide them, taking the time to understand these terms can help you avoid surprises and make more informed decisions.

One of the key components of closing is the final verification of your financial position. Lenders will confirm that your down payment funds are available and properly sourced, that your business and personal financials have not changed significantly, and that all required documentation is complete. This final review ensures that the risk profile of the loan remains consistent with what was approved. Any unexpected changes—such as large withdrawals, new debts, or declining revenue—can delay or even jeopardize closing, so maintaining financial stability during this period is critical.

Another important step is securing insurance coverage for the property. SBA lenders require borrowers to obtain adequate insurance, including property insurance and, in some cases, liability coverage. This protects both you and the lender in the event of damage or loss. The cost of insurance should be factored into your overall budget, as it becomes part of your ongoing operating expenses. Ensuring that coverage is in place before closing is a mandatory requirement and a key part of risk management. The title company or closing attorney plays a central role in the transaction. They conduct a title search to verify that the property is free of liens or legal issues that could affect ownership. They also prepare the closing statement, which details all financial aspects of the transaction, including the purchase price, loan amount, closing costs, and any credits or adjustments. Reviewing this statement carefully ensures that all numbers align with your expectations and that there are no discrepancies.

On the day of closing, you will sign all required documents and transfer your down payment and closing costs. Once the funds are disbursed and the transaction is recorded, ownership of the property is officially transferred to you. This moment marks the transition from tenant to owner—a shift that carries both financial benefits and new responsibilities. While the process may feel administrative, it represents a significant achievement and the beginning of a new phase in your business journey.

After closing, the focus shifts to transitioning your business operations into the new property. This may involve moving equipment, setting up utilities, and making any necessary modifications to the space. Planning this transition carefully can minimize disruptions and ensure a smooth start. Depending on your business, you may need to coordinate with vendors, employees, and customers to manage the move effectively. A well-executed transition can enhance productivity and set the tone for future success. One of the immediate financial changes after closing is the shift from rent payments to mortgage payments. While these payments may be similar in amount, their impact is fundamentally different. Mortgage payments contribute to equity, gradually increasing your ownership in the property. Over time, this equity becomes a valuable asset that can be leveraged for future opportunities. Understanding this shift helps reinforce the long-term value of ownership and encourages a strategic approach to financial management.

Another important consideration is budgeting for ongoing property expenses. In addition to your mortgage payment, you will now be responsible for property taxes, insurance, maintenance, and repairs. These costs must be factored into your financial planning to ensure that your business remains stable and profitable. Creating a detailed budget and setting aside reserves for unexpected expenses can help you manage these responsibilities effectively.

Ownership also provides opportunities for customization and improvement. Unlike a leased space, where modifications may be limited, owning your property allows you to tailor the environment to your business needs. This could include renovations, expansions, or upgrades that improve efficiency and customer experience. These improvements can enhance the value of the property and contribute to long-term growth.

Another strategic advantage of ownership is the potential to generate additional income. If your property includes extra space, you may be able to lease it to other businesses, creating a secondary revenue stream. This income can offset your mortgage costs and improve cash flow. Evaluating these opportunities and incorporating them into your strategy can further enhance the financial benefits of ownership.

As you settle into ownership, it is important to think long-term. Your property is not just a place of business—it is an asset that can play a central role in your financial future. Whether you plan to expand, refinance, or eventually sell, the decisions you make after closing will influence the value and performance of this asset. Maintaining the property, managing expenses, and monitoring market conditions are all part of this ongoing process.

Risk management continues to be important after closing. This includes maintaining adequate insurance, addressing maintenance issues promptly, and monitoring your financial performance. Being proactive in managing risks can prevent small issues from becoming larger problems and ensure that your investment remains secure.

Ultimately, closing the deal is not the end of the journey—it is the beginning of a new chapter. It is the point at which your planning and preparation become a tangible asset that supports your business and builds your wealth. By approaching this transition with a clear strategy and a long-term perspective, you can maximize the benefits of ownership and set the stage for continued success.

Real-Life Math Example: Closing Costs, Transition Expenses, and Long-Term Equity Growth

Let's walk through a detailed real-life example to understand the financial impact of closing and transitioning into ownership. Consider a business owner named Rachel who operates a growing childcare center. Rachel is currently leasing a facility for $7,000 per month and decides to purchase a property valued at $1,100,000 using an SBA loan.

Rachel secures financing with a 10% down payment of $110,000 and a loan amount of $990,000 at an interest rate of 7% over 25 years. Her monthly mortgage payment is approximately $7,000, which is equal to her current rent. At first glance, her monthly expense remains the same, but the financial implications are very different.

Now let's break down her closing costs. Rachel pays approximately $4,500 for an appraisal, $2,000 for an environmental report, $3,000 in legal and title fees, and $2,500 in lender fees. Her total closing costs amount to

$12,000. Combined with her down payment, her total upfront investment is $122,000.

After closing, Rachel incurs additional transition costs, including $15,000 for minor renovations, $5,000 for moving expenses, and $3,000 for new equipment setup. Her total transition costs are $23,000, bringing her total initial investment to $145,000.

Now let's analyze her monthly financial position. While her mortgage payment is $7,000, she now builds equity with each payment. In the first year, approximately $18,000 of her payments go toward principal reduction. This means that part of her monthly expense is effectively being converted into ownership.

Over 10 years, Rachel will pay approximately $840,000 in mortgage payments. During this time, she may reduce the principal by approximately $250,000. If the property appreciates at 3% annually, its value could increase from $1,100,000 to approximately $1,480,000, adding $380,000 in value.

This means that after 10 years, Rachel's total equity could exceed $630,000 when combining principal reduction and appreciation. In contrast, if she had continued leasing at $7,000 per month with a 3% annual increase, she would pay approximately $975,000 in rent over the same period with no equity gained.

Now consider the long-term impact over 25 years. Rachel will eventually pay off the loan and own the property outright. At that point, her monthly housing cost drops significantly, limited primarily to taxes, insurance, and maintenance. If the property continues to appreciate, it could be worth over $2 million, representing a substantial asset.

Additionally, Rachel has the option to lease a portion of the property to another business for $1,500 per month. This reduces her effective mortgage cost to $5,500, improving her cash flow and increasing her overall return on investment.

This example demonstrates how closing and transitioning into ownership impacts both short-term expenses and long-term wealth. While the upfront costs may seem significant, they are an investment in an asset that provides ongoing financial benefits. By understanding these numbers and planning accordingly, business owners can make the transition with confidence and position themselves for long-term success.

Chapter 8

Managing Your Owner-Occupied Property for Long-Term Success

Owning your business property through an SBA mortgage loan is not the end of the journey—it is the beginning of a new phase that requires discipline, strategy, and ongoing management. Many business owners focus intensely on getting approved and closing the deal, but the real long-term success comes from how the property is managed after acquisition. Proper management ensures that the property remains an asset that supports your business, builds equity, and generates opportunities, rather than becoming a financial burden. This chapter will guide you through the key principles of managing your owner-occupied commercial property effectively for long-term growth and stability.

The first shift that occurs after ownership is a change in mindset. As a tenant, your primary responsibility is paying rent and maintaining your leased space. As an owner, you are now responsible for the entire property, including maintenance, taxes, insurance, and long-term planning. This shift requires a proactive approach. Instead of reacting to issues, you must anticipate them, budget for them, and manage them strategically. This mindset is what separates successful property owners from those who struggle with unexpected expenses and inefficiencies.

One of the most important aspects of property management is maintenance. Regular maintenance protects the value of your asset and prevents small issues from becoming costly problems. This includes routine inspections, servicing HVAC systems, maintaining roofing and structural components, and ensuring that plumbing and electrical systems are functioning properly. Creating a maintenance schedule and setting aside funds for repairs can help you manage these responsibilities effectively. Preventive maintenance is almost always less expensive than reactive repairs, and it helps preserve the long-term value of the property.

Budgeting is another critical component of managing your property. In addition to your mortgage payment, you must account for property taxes, insurance, utilities, maintenance, and potential capital improvements. A well-structured budget allows you to plan for these expenses and avoid financial surprises. It also helps you evaluate the overall performance of your property and identify areas where costs can be controlled or reduced. Consistent budgeting ensures that your property remains financially sustainable and aligned with your business goals. Cash flow management is closely tied to budgeting. Even if your property is owner-occupied, it should be treated as a financial asset with its own income and expenses. If you have additional space that can be leased, that income should be tracked and managed separately. Monitoring cash flow allows you to assess the performance of the property and make informed decisions about improvements, refinancing, or expansion. Strong cash flow management is essential for maintaining financial stability and maximizing the return on your investment.

Another key factor in long-term success is property appreciation. While appreciation is influenced by market conditions, there are steps you can take to enhance the value of your property. This includes maintaining the property in excellent condition, making strategic improvements, and ensuring that it remains competitive within the local market. Upgrades such as modernizing interiors, improving energy efficiency, or enhancing curb appeal can increase both the usability and value of the property. These improvements not only benefit your business operations but also contribute to long-term equity growth.

Leverage is another powerful tool available to property owners. As you build equity in your property, you may have opportunities to refinance or access additional capital through lines of credit. This capital can be used to expand your business, acquire additional properties, or invest in other opportunities. Understanding how to use leverage responsibly is key to scaling your business and maximizing the value of your real estate assets. However, it is important to balance growth with risk management to avoid overextending your finances.

Risk management remains an ongoing responsibility after closing. This includes maintaining adequate insurance coverage, monitoring market conditions, and preparing for potential economic changes. Having a contingency plan and maintaining financial reserves can help you navigate unexpected challenges, such as downturns in business revenue or increases in operating costs. Proactive risk management ensures that your property remains a stable and reliable asset.

Another important aspect of property management is compliance. This includes adhering to local regulations, maintaining proper licensing, and ensuring that the property meets all safety and zoning requirements. Failure to comply with these regulations can result in fines, legal issues, or operational disruptions. Staying informed and working with professionals when necessary can help you maintain compliance and avoid unnecessary complications.

As your business grows, your property should evolve with it. This may involve expanding your space, reconfiguring layouts, or even acquiring additional properties. Strategic planning is essential to ensure that your real estate supports your long-term goals. Regularly evaluating your property's performance and aligning it with your business strategy allows you to make informed decisions and capitalize on opportunities.

Exit strategy planning is another important consideration. While ownership provides long-term benefits, there may come a time when you decide to sell your property or transition your business. Having a clear exit strategy allows you to maximize the value of your investment and achieve your financial goals. This could involve selling the property, leasing it to another business, or incorporating it into a larger portfolio strategy. Planning ahead ensures that you are prepared for these decisions when the time comes.

Technology and systems can also play a role in effective property management. Using tools to track expenses, schedule maintenance, and monitor performance can improve efficiency and reduce the likelihood of errors. These systems provide valuable insights that help you manage your property more effectively and make data-driven decisions.

Ultimately, managing your owner-occupied commercial property is about creating a balance between operational efficiency and long-term investment growth. It requires attention to detail, strategic planning, and a commitment to maintaining the value of your asset. By approaching property management with the same level of discipline and focus that you apply to your business, you can ensure that your investment continues to support your success for years to come.

Real-Life Math Example: Long-Term Management, Cash Flow, and Equity Growth

Let's walk through a detailed real-life scenario to illustrate how managing an owner-occupied property impacts financial performance over time. Consider a business owner named Michael who operates a successful printing company. Michael purchased a commercial property for $1,200,000 using an SBA loan with a 10% down payment of $120,000 and a loan amount of $1,080,000 at 7% interest over 25 years. His monthly mortgage payment is approximately $7,650.

In addition to his mortgage, Michael has annual property taxes of $18,000, insurance costs of $6,000, and maintenance expenses averaging $12,000 per year. This brings his total annual property expenses to approximately $127,800, or $10,650 per month. While this is higher than his previous rent of $9,500 per month, the key difference is that a portion of his mortgage payment is building equity.

In the first year, Michael pays approximately $91,800 in mortgage payments, with about $20,000 going toward principal reduction. This means that his effective cost, after accounting for equity gained, is closer to $71,800. When combined with his other expenses, his adjusted annual cost is approximately $107,800, or about $8,983 per month—actually lower than his previous rent when considering equity.

Now let's consider additional income. Michael leases out a portion of his property to a small business for $2,000 per month, generating $24,000 annually. This reduces his net annual cost to approximately $83,800, or about $6,983 per month. This significantly improves his cash flow and makes ownership more advantageous than leasing.

Over 10 years, Michael will pay approximately $918,000 in mortgage payments. During this time, he may reduce the principal by approximately $300,000. If the property appreciates at 3% annually, its value could increase to approximately $1,610,000, adding $410,000 in value.

This means that after 10 years, Michael's total equity could exceed $710,000 when combining principal reduction and appreciation. In contrast, if he had continued leasing at $9,500 per month with a 3% annual increase, he would pay approximately $1.3 million in rent with no equity gained.

Now consider the long-term impact over 25 years. Once the loan is paid off, Michael's monthly costs drop significantly, limited to taxes, insurance, and maintenance. If these costs total $3,000 per month, and he continues to generate $2,000 per month in rental income, his net cost drops to just $1,000 per month. This represents a dramatic improvement compared to his original rent.

Additionally, the property may be worth over $2 million at this point, providing a substantial asset that can be sold, refinanced, or passed on as part of a long-term wealth strategy.

This example demonstrates how effective property management, combined with strategic planning, can transform a commercial property into a powerful financial asset. By controlling expenses, generating additional income, and maintaining the property's value, business owners can maximize their return and build lasting wealth.

Chapter 9

Refinancing, Leveraging Equity, and Scaling Your Business with SBA Mortgage Loans

Once you have successfully acquired and stabilized your owner-occupied commercial property, a new set of opportunities begins to emerge. Ownership is not just about reducing rent or building equity—it is about creating leverage that can be used to grow your business, expand your portfolio, and increase your overall financial power. Many business owners stop at acquisition, but the most successful ones understand how to strategically refinance, access equity, and redeploy capital to accelerate growth. This chapter focuses on how to take your initial SBA-financed property and turn it into a long-term engine for expansion and wealth creation.

Refinancing is one of the most powerful tools available to property owners. Over time, as you pay down your loan and your property appreciates, you build equity. Refinancing allows you to tap into that equity by replacing your existing loan with a new one, often with better terms or a higher loan amount. This can result in lower monthly payments, improved cash flow, or access to capital that can be used for other investments. Understanding when and how to refinance is critical to maximizing the value of your property.

One of the most common reasons to refinance is to lower your interest rate. If market rates decrease or your financial profile improves, you may be able to secure a lower rate than your original loan. Even a small reduction in interest rate can result in significant savings over the life of the loan. Lower payments improve cash flow, which can be reinvested into your business or used to build reserves. Timing your refinance to take advantage of favorable market conditions can have a substantial impact on your long-term financial performance.

Another reason to refinance is to change the structure of your loan. For example, you may transition from a variable-rate SBA 7(a) loan to a more stable structure, or you may extend your amortization period to reduce monthly payments. These adjustments can improve your financial flexibility and make it easier to manage your property over time. However, it is important to carefully evaluate the costs of refinancing, including fees and potential prepayment penalties, to ensure that the benefits outweigh the costs.

Cash-out refinancing is another strategy that allows you to access the equity you have built in your property. In this scenario, you refinance your existing loan for a higher amount than your current balance and receive the difference in cash. This capital can be used to expand your business, purchase additional properties, or invest in new opportunities. Cash-out refinancing effectively turns your property into a source of funding, allowing you to leverage your existing asset to create new income streams.

Leveraging equity requires a strategic approach. While it can accelerate growth, it also increases your financial obligations. It is important to ensure that any new investments or expansions generate sufficient returns to justify the additional debt. Careful planning and analysis are essential to avoid over-leveraging and to maintain financial stability. Successful business owners use leverage as a tool, not a crutch, balancing growth with risk management.

Another way to leverage your property is through lines of credit or secondary financing. As your equity increases, lenders may be willing to provide additional financing secured by your property. This can offer flexibility and quick access to capital without the need for a full refinance. Lines of credit can be particularly useful for short-term needs, such as covering operating expenses, funding renovations, or taking advantage of time-sensitive opportunities. Scaling your business often involves expanding into new locations or increasing capacity. Your owner-occupied property can play a central role in this process. For example, you may use the equity in your current property to fund the purchase of a second location. Alternatively, you may expand your existing property to accommodate growth. Understanding how to integrate your real estate strategy with your business expansion plans is key to achieving sustainable growth.

Another important consideration is the potential to transition your property from owner-occupied to partially or fully leased. As your business evolves, you may outgrow your current space or relocate to a larger facility. In this case, your original property can become an income-generating asset. Leasing it to other businesses creates a new revenue stream and allows you to benefit from both rental income and continued appreciation. This transition can significantly enhance your overall financial position.

Tax strategy also plays a role in refinancing and leveraging equity. While specific tax implications should be discussed with a professional, refinancing and property ownership can offer opportunities for deductions and strategic planning. Understanding how these factors impact your overall financial picture can help you make more informed decisions and maximize your returns. Market conditions are another critical factor in refinancing and scaling decisions. Interest rates, property values, and economic trends all influence the feasibility and timing of these strategies. Staying informed about market conditions allows you to act at the right time and take advantage of opportunities as they arise. Being proactive rather than reactive is key to successful long-term planning.

Risk management remains essential as you scale. Increasing your leverage and expanding your operations introduces new risks, including higher debt obligations and greater exposure to market fluctuations. Maintaining strong cash reserves, monitoring your financial performance, and planning for potential challenges can help you manage these risks effectively.

Ultimately, refinancing and leveraging equity are about turning your property into a dynamic asset that supports your long-term goals. By understanding how to use these tools strategically, you can move beyond ownership and begin building a portfolio of assets that generate income, support your business, and create lasting wealth.

Real-Life Math Example: Refinancing, Cash-Out Equity, and Scaling Growth

Let's walk through a detailed real-life scenario to illustrate how refinancing and leveraging equity can impact long-term financial outcomes. Consider a business owner named Steven who owns a commercial property purchased for $1,000,000 using an SBA loan with a 10% down payment of $100,000. His original loan amount was $900,000 at a 7% interest rate over 25 years, resulting in a monthly payment of approximately $6,360.

After 7 years, Steven has paid down his loan balance to approximately $750,000. During this time, the property has appreciated at an average rate of 3% per year, increasing its value to approximately $1,230,000. This means Steven now has approximately $480,000 in equity ($1,230,000 minus $750,000).

Steven decides to refinance his property. He qualifies for a new loan at 6% interest and chooses to refinance up to 75% of the property's current value. This results in a new loan amount of approximately $922,500 (75% of $1,230,000). After paying off his existing balance of $750,000, Steven receives approximately $172,500 in cash.

His new loan has a monthly payment of approximately $5,530, which is lower than his original payment due to the reduced interest rate and re-amortization. This improves his monthly cash flow while also providing him with a significant amount of capital.

Steven uses the $172,500 to fund the purchase of a second property valued at $800,000, using it as a 20% down payment. He secures financing for the remaining $640,000 and generates rental income of $6,000 per month from this new property.

Now let's analyze the financial impact. Steven's original property continues to generate value and appreciation, while his new property produces rental income. Over the next 10 years, if both properties appreciate at 3% annually, the original property could be worth approximately $1,650,000, and the new property could be worth approximately $1,070,000.

Additionally, Steven continues to pay down both loans, building equity in both properties. Combined, his total equity could exceed $1 million after 10 years, depending on loan amortization and market conditions.

If Steven had not refinanced and leveraged his equity, he would have continued building equity in a single property but would not have been able to acquire a second asset. By using refinancing strategically, he accelerates his wealth-building process and creates multiple income streams.

This example demonstrates how refinancing and leveraging equity can transform a single property into a foundation for broader financial growth. By understanding these strategies and applying them effectively, business owners can move beyond ownership and begin building a portfolio that supports long-term success.

Chapter 10

Advanced Strategies for Building Wealth with Owner-Occupied SBA Commercial Real Estate

Reaching the point where you understand how to acquire, finance, and manage an owner-occupied commercial property is a major achievement. However, the most successful business owners do not stop there. They evolve from simply owning a property into strategically using that property as a foundation to build long-term wealth, multiple income streams, and financial independence. This chapter focuses on advanced strategies that take everything you have learned throughout this series and elevate it into a comprehensive wealth-building system using SBA commercial real estate.

The first advanced strategy is thinking in terms of portfolio building rather than single-property ownership. Many business owners purchase one property and remain there indefinitely, missing the opportunity to scale. Instead, your first owner-occupied property should be viewed as the starting point of a larger portfolio. By leveraging equity, improving your financial profile, and gaining experience with SBA financing, you position yourself to acquire additional properties over time. Each acquisition builds on the previous one, creating a compounding effect that accelerates wealth creation.

A key component of this strategy is transitioning from pure owner-occupancy to a hybrid model. Initially, your property must meet SBA occupancy requirements, but as your business grows, you may expand into new locations or require different types of space. When this happens, your original property can shift from being fully owner-occupied to partially leased or even fully leased. This transition allows you to convert your operational space into an income-producing asset while maintaining ownership. Over time, this can create a portfolio of properties that generate consistent rental income.

Another advanced strategy is value-add investing within owner-occupied properties. This involves identifying opportunities to increase the value of your property through improvements, better utilization of space, or operational efficiencies. For example, renovating unused areas, upgrading facilities, or reconfiguring layouts can increase both the usability and market value of the property. These improvements not only enhance your business operations but also increase the equity and potential resale value of the asset.

Strategic refinancing plays a central role in advanced wealth-building. As discussed in the previous chapter, refinancing allows you to access the equity in your property. At an advanced level, this becomes a repeatable strategy. You acquire a property, improve its value, allow it to appreciate, refinance to extract equity, and then reinvest that capital into new opportunities. This cycle can be repeated multiple times, creating exponential growth in your portfolio. The key is to manage this process carefully, ensuring that each step is financially sustainable.

Another important concept is diversification. While commercial real estate can be a powerful asset, relying solely on one property or one type of business can increase risk. Advanced investors diversify by acquiring different types of properties, operating in different markets, or investing in complementary assets. For example, you may own an owner-occupied office building, a rental retail property, and an industrial warehouse. This diversification reduces risk and creates multiple streams of income.

Tax strategy becomes increasingly important as your portfolio grows. Commercial real estate offers various tax advantages, including depreciation and potential deductions related to interest and operating expenses. At an advanced level, understanding how to structure your ownership, manage your income, and plan for tax efficiency can significantly impact your overall returns. Working with experienced professionals can help you optimize these strategies and maximize your financial outcomes.

Another advanced strategy is integrating your real estate with your overall business exit plan. Many business owners focus on building their business but overlook the role that real estate can play in their eventual exit. Owning your property gives you flexibility when it comes time to sell your business. You can sell the business and retain ownership of the property, creating ongoing rental income, or you can package the business and property together to increase the overall sale value. Planning for this in advance allows you to maximize your return when you decide to exit.

Partnerships and joint ventures are also tools that can accelerate growth. While many SBA loans require majority ownership, there are ways to structure partnerships that align with SBA guidelines while allowing you to leverage additional capital and expertise. Partnering with other investors or operators can enable you to take on larger projects and expand more quickly than you could on your own. However, these arrangements must be structured carefully to ensure alignment and compliance.

Another advanced concept is repositioning properties for higher value uses. As markets evolve, the highest and best use of a property may change. For example, a property that was originally used for office space may become more valuable as a medical facility or mixed-use development. Recognizing these opportunities and repositioning your property accordingly can significantly increase its value and income potential.

Technology and data analysis also play a role in advanced real estate strategies. Monitoring market trends, analyzing property performance, and using data to guide decisions can provide a competitive advantage. This allows you to identify opportunities, optimize operations, and make informed investment decisions.

Risk management becomes even more critical at this stage. As your portfolio grows, so does your exposure to market fluctuations, economic changes, and operational challenges. Maintaining strong financial reserves, monitoring your leverage, and diversifying your assets are all essential to managing these risks. Advanced investors focus not only on growth but also on preserving and protecting their wealth.

Ultimately, the goal of these advanced strategies is to create a system where your properties work together to support your financial goals. Your owner-occupied property becomes the foundation, and each additional step builds on that foundation. By combining acquisition, management, refinancing, and strategic planning, you can create a portfolio that generates income, builds equity, and provides long-term financial security.

Real-Life Math Example: Building a Multi-Property Portfolio Using SBA Financing

Let's walk through a comprehensive real-life example to illustrate how these advanced strategies can be applied over time. Consider a business owner named Carlos who starts with a single owner-occupied property purchased for $1,000,000 using an SBA loan with a 10% down payment of $100,000. His loan amount is $900,000 at 7% interest over 25 years, resulting in a monthly payment of approximately $6,360.

After 5 years, Carlos has paid down his loan balance to approximately $820,000, and the property has appreciated to $1,160,000. This gives him approximately $340,000 in equity. He decides to refinance and extract $150,000 in cash while maintaining a manageable loan balance.

Carlos uses this $150,000 as a down payment on a second property valued at $750,000. This property generates rental income of $5,500 per month, while his mortgage payment is approximately $4,800, creating positive cash flow of $700 per month. Over the next 5 years, both properties continue to appreciate at 3% annually. The first property increases in value to approximately $1,340,000, while the second property increases to approximately $870,000. Carlos also continues to pay down both loans, building additional equity.

At this point, Carlos owns two properties with a combined value of over $2.2 million. His total equity may exceed $700,000 when combining appreciation and principal reduction. He now has multiple income streams, including his business income and rental income from the second property.

Carlos then repeats the process. He refinances again, extracts additional equity, and uses it to acquire a third property. Over time, this cycle continues, and his portfolio grows to include multiple properties generating consistent income.

Now let's compare this to a scenario where Carlos only owns one property. While he would still build equity, his growth would be significantly slower, and he would not benefit from multiple income streams. By leveraging his initial investment and applying advanced strategies, he accelerates his wealth-building process.

Over a 20-year period, Carlos's portfolio could grow to include properties worth several million dollars, generating substantial rental income and providing long-term financial security. His original owner-occupied property serves as the foundation for this entire system.

This example demonstrates how advanced strategies can transform a single SBA-financed property into a powerful wealth-building engine. By understanding and applying these concepts, business owners can move beyond basic ownership and create a scalable, sustainable path to financial independence.

Chapter 11

Avoiding Costly Mistakes in SBA Owner-Occupied Commercial Real Estate

As powerful as SBA owner-occupied commercial real estate can be for building wealth and stability, it is equally important to understand the mistakes that can derail progress, reduce profitability, or even lead to financial distress. Many business owners enter the process with strong intentions but lack the experience to identify risks early. The difference between long-term success and costly setbacks often comes down to avoiding a handful of critical errors. This chapter is designed to help you recognize, prevent, and strategically navigate the most common mistakes in SBA commercial property ownership.

One of the most common and dangerous mistakes is overpaying for a property. In competitive markets, business owners may feel pressure to secure a location quickly and end up paying above market value. This can create immediate challenges during the appraisal process, potentially requiring additional cash to close or forcing renegotiation. More importantly, overpaying reduces your equity position from day one and limits your ability to refinance or leverage the property in the future. Conducting thorough market analysis and relying on comparable sales is essential to ensuring that your purchase price aligns with true market value.

Another major mistake is underestimating total ownership costs. Many borrowers focus primarily on the mortgage payment and overlook additional expenses such as property taxes, insurance, maintenance, utilities, and capital improvements. These costs can add up quickly and impact your cash flow. Without proper budgeting, a property that initially appears affordable can become a financial strain. Successful property owners take a comprehensive approach to cost analysis, ensuring that all expenses are accounted for and that sufficient reserves are maintained.

Poor deal structuring is another common issue that can lead to loan denial or unfavorable terms. This includes insufficient down payment, weak debt service coverage ratio (DSCR), or improperly documented financials. Even a strong business can face challenges if the deal is not structured correctly. Working with experienced professionals and understanding lender expectations can help you avoid these pitfalls and position your application for approval.

Lack of financial reserves is another critical mistake. Owning a commercial property requires the ability to handle unexpected expenses, such as repairs, temporary revenue declines, or economic changes. Without adequate reserves, even minor issues can escalate into major problems. Lenders often require reserves as part of the approval process, but it is equally important for borrowers to maintain their own safety net. Having several months of operating expenses set aside provides stability and confidence.

Another mistake is failing to plan for future growth. Some business owners purchase properties that meet their immediate needs but lack the flexibility to accommodate expansion. This can lead to the need for relocation sooner than expected, which can be costly and disruptive. Evaluating properties with a long-term perspective—considering future space requirements and growth potential—can help you avoid this issue and maximize the value of your investment.

Inadequate due diligence is another area where mistakes can occur. Skipping or rushing inspections, environmental assessments, or property evaluations can result in hidden problems that surface after closing. These issues can be expensive to fix and may impact your ability to operate your business effectively. Taking the time to conduct thorough due diligence and address any concerns before closing is essential to protecting your investment.

Another common error is misunderstanding loan terms and obligations. SBA loans come with specific requirements, including occupancy rules, personal guarantees, and potential prepayment penalties. Failing to fully understand these terms can lead to unexpected challenges down the line. Reviewing loan documents carefully and asking questions ensures that you are fully aware of your obligations and can plan accordingly.

Overleveraging is another risk that can undermine long-term success. While leveraging equity can accelerate growth, taking on too much debt without sufficient income to support it can create financial stress. Balancing growth with sustainability is key. Each new investment should be evaluated carefully to ensure that it strengthens your overall financial position rather than weakening it.

Another mistake is neglecting property management after closing. Some business owners assume that ownership requires little ongoing effort, but this is far from the truth. Failing to maintain the property, monitor expenses, or plan for improvements can lead to declining value and increased costs. Active management is essential to preserving and enhancing your investment.

Market timing is another factor that can impact your success.

While it is impossible to predict market conditions perfectly, making decisions without considering interest rates, economic trends, and property values can lead to suboptimal outcomes. Staying informed and working with knowledgeable professionals can help you make more strategic decisions.

Another critical mistake is failing to align your real estate strategy with your overall business goals. Your property should support your operations, enhance efficiency, and contribute to your long-term vision. If the property does not align with your business strategy, it can create operational challenges and limit your growth potential. Integrating your real estate decisions with your business planning ensures that both work together effectively.

Communication breakdowns during the loan process can also create problems. Delays in responding to lender requests, incomplete documentation, or misunderstandings can slow down the process and increase stress. Maintaining clear and consistent communication with all parties involved helps ensure a smoother transaction.

Finally, one of the biggest mistakes is not taking action due to fear or uncertainty. While it is important to be cautious and informed, excessive hesitation can result in missed opportunities. SBA owner-occupied financing provides a powerful pathway to ownership and wealth building, but it requires commitment and confidence. Educating yourself and working with experienced professionals can help you overcome these barriers and move forward.

Avoiding these mistakes is not about perfection—it is about awareness and preparation. By understanding the potential pitfalls and taking proactive steps to address them, you can navigate the process more effectively and position yourself for long-term success.

Real-Life Math Example: The Cost of Mistakes vs Strategic Decision-Making

Let's walk through a detailed real-life scenario to illustrate how common mistakes can impact financial outcomes. Consider two business owners, James and Olivia, who both operate similar businesses and are looking to purchase commercial properties.

James purchases a property for $1,200,000 without conducting thorough market analysis. The appraisal comes in at $1,100,000, meaning he overpaid by $100,000. To close the deal, he must increase his down payment from $120,000 to $220,000. His loan amount remains $1,080,000, and his monthly payment is approximately $7,650.

In addition, James underestimates his annual property expenses. He budgets $20,000 for taxes, insurance, and maintenance but ends up paying $30,000. This adds an extra $833 per month to his expenses, bringing his total monthly cost to approximately $8,483.

Now consider Olivia, who purchases a similar property for $1,150,000 after negotiating based on comparable sales. Her appraisal matches the purchase price, and she invests a 10% down payment of $115,000. Her loan amount is $1,035,000, with a monthly payment of approximately $7,300.

Olivia also budgets accurately for her expenses, setting aside $30,000 annually. Her total monthly cost is approximately $9,800, including all expenses, but she leases a portion of her property for $2,000 per month, reducing her net cost to $7,800.

Over 10 years, James pays approximately $918,000 in mortgage payments and builds around $300,000 in equity. However, his initial overpayment and higher expenses reduce his overall financial position. His property appreciates to approximately $1,610,000, but his total equity is lower due to the higher starting cost.

Olivia, on the other hand, pays approximately $876,000 in mortgage payments and builds a similar amount of equity.

However, her lower purchase price and additional rental income improve her cash flow and overall returns. Her property also appreciates to a similar value, but her equity position is stronger due to better initial structuring. Now consider the impact of reserves. James did not maintain sufficient reserves and faces a $20,000 repair in year three, which he finances with high-interest debt. Olivia had reserves set aside and covers the expense without additional debt.

This example demonstrates how small differences in decision-making can have significant long-term effects. Overpaying, underestimating expenses, and failing to plan can reduce profitability and increase risk. On the other hand, careful analysis, proper budgeting, and strategic planning can enhance returns and create a more stable financial position.

By understanding these dynamics and avoiding common mistakes, business owners can make smarter decisions and fully realize the benefits of SBA owner-occupied commercial real estate.

Chapter 12

Building a Long-Term Exit Strategy with Owner-Occupied SBA Commercial Real Estate

Owning an owner-occupied commercial property through SBA financing is not just about solving today's operational needs—it is about positioning yourself for a powerful long-term exit. The most successful business owners do not wait until the end of their journey to think about their exit strategy; they design it from the moment they acquire their property. Your commercial real estate can play a central role in how you retire, sell your business, generate passive income, or transfer wealth to future generations. This chapter focuses on how to strategically build and execute a long-term exit plan using the foundation you have created through SBA owner-occupied property ownership.

The first step in building an exit strategy is understanding that your business and your real estate are two separate but interconnected assets. Many business owners treat them as one, but separating them creates flexibility and control. When your business operates from a property owned by a separate entity, you gain options. You can sell the business while retaining ownership of the property, lease the property to the new owner, or sell both together as a package. This flexibility allows you to structure your exit in a way that maximizes value and aligns with your financial goals.

One of the most common and effective exit strategies is selling the business while keeping the real estate. In this scenario, you transition from an active business owner to a passive landlord. The buyer of your business becomes your tenant, paying rent that provides ongoing income. This creates a stable cash flow stream while allowing you to step away from daily operations. Over time, this rental income can replace or even exceed the income you previously earned from the business itself.

Another strategy is selling both the business and the real estate together. This approach can increase the overall value of the transaction, particularly if the property is integral to the business operations. Buyers often see added value in owning the real estate along with the business, as it provides stability and control. Packaging these assets together can attract higher-quality buyers and result in a larger payout at closing. However, this strategy requires careful planning to ensure that both assets are positioned effectively for sale.

Refinancing also plays a role in exit planning. As you build equity in your property, you may choose to refinance and extract capital before selling your business. This allows you to access a portion of your wealth without giving up ownership. The funds can be used for diversification, retirement planning, or other investments. This strategy provides liquidity while maintaining your position in the real estate asset.

Leasing your property to third-party tenants is another option, particularly if your business relocates or ceases operations. In this case, your property becomes a fully income-producing asset. The rental income can provide consistent cash flow and long-term financial security. This strategy requires understanding the local rental market, setting competitive lease rates, and managing tenant relationships effectively.

Timing is a critical factor in any exit strategy. Market conditions, interest rates, and economic trends all influence the value of your property and business. Selling during a strong market can significantly increase your returns, while poor timing can reduce your overall outcome. Monitoring market conditions and planning your exit accordingly allows you to capitalize on favorable opportunities.

Tax planning is another essential component of exit strategy. The way you structure your sale—whether it involves the business, the real estate, or both—can have significant tax implications. Understanding how to minimize taxes and maximize net proceeds is critical to achieving your financial goals. Working with experienced professionals can help you navigate these complexities and develop a strategy that aligns with your objectives.

Another important consideration is succession planning. If you intend to pass your business or property to family members or partners, having a clear plan in place ensures a smooth transition. This includes defining ownership structures, outlining responsibilities, and preparing successors to manage the assets effectively. A well-structured succession plan preserves value and reduces the risk of conflict or disruption.

Diversification is also a key element of long-term planning. While your owner-occupied property may be a significant asset, relying solely on one property or one business can increase risk. As you approach your exit, consider diversifying your investments into other asset classes, such as additional real estate, financial investments, or passive income streams. This creates a more balanced portfolio and enhances financial security.

Another advanced strategy is leveraging your property for partial exits. Instead of selling everything at once, you may choose to sell a portion of your business or property while retaining some ownership. This allows you to realize some of your gains while still participating in future growth. Partial exits can provide flexibility and reduce risk while maintaining upside potential.

Emotional readiness is also an important factor in exit planning. Selling a business or transitioning away from ownership can be a significant life change. Preparing mentally and financially for this transition ensures that you are ready to move forward and make decisions that align with your long-term vision.

Ultimately, your exit strategy should be aligned with your personal and financial goals. Whether you aim to generate passive income, achieve a large payout, or create a legacy for your family, your commercial property can be a powerful tool in achieving those objectives. By planning ahead and understanding your options, you can maximize the value of your investment and create a successful transition.

Real-Life Math Example: Exit Strategies and Long-Term Wealth Outcomes

Let's walk through a detailed real-life scenario to illustrate how different exit strategies impact financial outcomes. Consider a business owner named Daniel who purchased a commercial property for $1,200,000 using an SBA loan with a

10% down payment of $120,000. His loan amount was $1,080,000 at 7% interest over 25 years, resulting in a monthly payment of approximately $7,650.

After 15 years, Daniel has paid down his loan balance to approximately $600,000. During this time, the property has appreciated at an average rate of 3% per year, increasing its value to approximately $1,870,000. This means Daniel now has approximately $1,270,000 in equity.

Now let's explore different exit scenarios. In the first scenario, Daniel sells both his business and the property together for $2,500,000. After paying off his remaining loan balance of $600,000, he receives $1,900,000 before taxes. This represents a significant return on his initial investment of $120,000.

In the second scenario, Daniel sells his business for $1,200,000 but retains ownership of the property. He leases the property to the new business owner for $12,000 per month, generating $144,000 annually. After accounting for expenses of $40,000 per year, his net income is $104,000 annually. Over 10 years, this generates over $1 million in income, while he still owns the property, which continues to appreciate.

In the third scenario, Daniel refinances the property before selling his business. He extracts $500,000 in cash through refinancing and uses it to invest in other opportunities. He then sells his business and continues to lease the property to a tenant. This allows him to access capital while maintaining ownership and income.

Now compare these scenarios to continuing to operate the business without an exit strategy. While Daniel would continue to earn income, he would not realize the full value of his assets or create the same level of financial flexibility.

This example demonstrates how strategic planning can significantly impact long-term outcomes. By understanding and evaluating different exit options, business owners can choose the path that best aligns with their goals and maximize the value of their investments.

Your owner-occupied commercial property is more than just a place to run your business—it is a cornerstone of your financial future. By building a thoughtful and strategic exit plan, you can transform that asset into lasting wealth, stability, and opportunity.

Chapter 13

Creating Generational Wealth Through Owner-Occupied SBA Commercial Real Estate

The ultimate goal for many business owners is not just financial success during their lifetime, but the ability to create lasting wealth that extends beyond them—wealth that supports their family, provides opportunities for future generations, and establishes a legacy of financial independence. Owner-occupied commercial real estate, when leveraged properly through SBA mortgage financing, can become one of the most powerful tools for achieving this goal. This chapter focuses on how to transform a single property into a generational wealth strategy that continues to grow and provide value long after the original acquisition.

Generational wealth begins with ownership. When you own your business property, you are not just controlling your operating environment—you are building an asset that can appreciate, generate income, and be passed down or transferred strategically. Unlike income from a job or even a business that may depend on active involvement, real estate has the potential to produce passive income and long-term appreciation. This combination makes it uniquely suited for creating wealth that endures across generations.

One of the foundational principles of generational wealth is consistency. Building wealth through commercial real estate is not about quick wins or short-term gains—it is about steady growth over time. Each mortgage payment reduces your debt and increases your equity. Each year of appreciation adds to the value of your asset. Over time, these incremental gains compound into significant wealth. Understanding and committing to this long-term perspective is essential to achieving lasting success.

Another key principle is control. Owning your property gives you control over how it is used, managed, and transferred. This control allows you to make decisions that align with your long-term goals, rather than being subject to the decisions of landlords or market fluctuations in rental agreements. Control also enables you to structure your ownership in ways that protect your assets and facilitate smooth transitions to future generations.

Estate planning plays a central role in creating generational wealth. Properly structuring your ownership and planning for the transfer of assets ensures that your property can be passed down efficiently and with minimal disruption. This may involve creating trusts, defining ownership interests, and establishing clear guidelines for management and distribution. While the specifics will vary based on individual circumstances, the goal is to preserve the value of your assets and ensure that they continue to benefit your family.

Another important aspect of generational wealth is education. Passing down assets without passing down knowledge can lead to mismanagement and loss of value. Teaching the next generation how to manage property, understand finances, and make strategic decisions is just as important as the assets themselves. This includes involving family members in the management process, sharing financial insights, and creating a culture of responsibility and stewardship.

Diversification is also critical in building generational wealth. While your owner-occupied property may serve as the foundation, expanding into additional properties or complementary investments can enhance stability and growth. Multiple assets provide multiple streams of income and reduce reliance on any single source. This diversification strengthens your overall financial position and creates a more resilient portfolio.

Another powerful strategy is reinvestment. Instead of extracting and spending the value created by your property, reinvesting that value into additional opportunities can accelerate growth. This may involve acquiring new properties, expanding existing ones, or investing in other ventures. Reinvestment allows your wealth to compound over time, creating exponential growth rather than linear progress.

Leverage continues to play a role in generational wealth building. By using financing strategically, you can acquire assets with less upfront capital and maximize your return on investment. However, leverage must be used responsibly, balancing growth with risk management. Maintaining a strong financial foundation and avoiding excessive debt ensures that your portfolio remains stable and sustainable.

Another consideration is income stability. Properties that generate consistent rental income can provide a reliable source of cash flow for future generations. This income can support living expenses, fund education, or be reinvested for further growth. Structuring your properties to maximize income potential—such as leasing unused space or transitioning to full rental use—enhances their long-term value.

Market awareness is also important. Understanding economic trends, property values, and market demand allows you to make informed decisions about when to buy, sell, or hold assets. Staying informed helps you protect your wealth and capitalize on opportunities as they arise.

Another advanced strategy is creating a family business or holding company that manages your real estate portfolio. This structure can centralize management, streamline decision-making, and provide a framework for involving multiple family members. It also allows for more efficient scaling and coordination as your portfolio grows.

Legacy planning goes beyond financial considerations. It involves defining your values, goals, and vision for how your wealth will be used and managed. This includes setting expectations for future generations, establishing guidelines for decision-making, and creating a shared understanding of the purpose behind your assets. A clear legacy plan ensures that your wealth continues to serve its intended purpose.

Risk management remains a constant throughout this process. Protecting your assets from unforeseen events, maintaining adequate insurance, and planning for economic downturns are all essential to preserving wealth. A strong risk management strategy ensures that your assets remain secure and continue to provide value over time.

Ultimately, creating generational wealth through owner-occupied SBA commercial real estate is about building something that lasts. It is about transforming a single investment into a system that supports your family, creates opportunities, and provides financial security for years to come. By applying the principles outlined in this chapter, you can turn your property into a lasting legacy.

Real-Life Math Example: Building and Passing Down a Multi-Generational Real Estate Portfolio

Let's walk through a detailed real-life scenario to illustrate how generational wealth can be built and sustained through owner-occupied commercial real estate. Consider a business owner named Victor who purchases a property for $1,000,000 using an SBA loan with a 10% down payment of $100,000. His loan amount is $900,000 at 7% interest over 25 years, resulting in a monthly payment of approximately $6,360.

Over 25 years, Victor pays off the loan completely. During this time, the property appreciates at an average rate of 3% annually, increasing its value to approximately $2,090,000. By the time the loan is paid off, Victor owns the property outright and has over $2 million in equity.

Now consider the income potential. Victor leases the property to a tenant for $12,000 per month, generating $144,000 annually. After accounting for expenses of $40,000 per year, his net income is $104,000 annually. This income continues indefinitely, providing a stable financial foundation. Victor then uses the equity in his property to acquire a second property during his ownership period. Over time, he builds a portfolio of three properties, each generating income and appreciating in value. By the time he is ready to retire, his portfolio is worth over $5 million and generates over $250,000 in annual income.

Now consider the transfer to the next generation. Victor structures his assets through a holding company and establishes a plan for his children to manage the properties. The income from the properties supports the family, while the assets continue to appreciate.

Over the next 20 years, the portfolio grows further. If the properties continue to appreciate at 3% annually, the total value could exceed $9 million. The rental income also increases with market rates, providing even greater financial stability.

Compare this to a scenario where Victor only earns income from his business without investing in real estate. While he may achieve financial success, the lack of appreciating assets and passive income limits his ability to create lasting wealth.

This example demonstrates how a single property, when managed and leveraged effectively, can evolve into a multi-generational portfolio. By focusing on long-term growth, reinvestment, and strategic planning, business owners can create wealth that extends far beyond their own lifetime.

Your journey with owner-occupied SBA commercial real estate does not end with ownership—it begins there. By applying the principles of generational wealth, you can transform your investment into a legacy that benefits not only you but also the generations that follow.

Chapter 14

Creating a Repeatable System for SBA Commercial Real Estate Success

At this stage in your journey, you have learned how to qualify for SBA financing, structure deals, acquire properties, manage them, leverage equity, scale your portfolio, and build toward long-term wealth and generational impact. The final step is transforming everything you have learned into a repeatable, scalable system. Success in SBA commercial real estate is not about a single transaction—it is about building a process that can be executed consistently over time. When you have a system, you remove guesswork, reduce risk, and create a predictable pathway to growth.

A repeatable system begins with clarity of strategy. You must define your target property types, ideal price range, preferred loan structures, and long-term goals. Without this clarity, every deal becomes a new decision, increasing complexity and reducing efficiency. With a defined strategy, you can evaluate opportunities quickly and focus only on those that align with your objectives. This allows you to move faster and with greater confidence. The next component of a system is deal sourcing. Successful investors do not wait for opportunities—they create pipelines. This includes working with commercial real estate agents, building relationships with lenders, networking with business owners, and monitoring listings regularly. Over time, you develop a consistent flow of potential deals, allowing you to be selective and strategic. A strong pipeline ensures that you are never dependent on a single opportunity.

Once deals are identified, the evaluation process must be standardized. This means using consistent criteria to analyze properties, including price, location, cash flow potential, DSCR, and long-term value. By applying the same framework to every deal, you can compare opportunities objectively and avoid emotional decision-making. This disciplined approach increases the likelihood of making sound investments.

Financing is another critical part of your system. Building relationships with SBA lenders and understanding their requirements allows you to move quickly when opportunities arise. Having prequalification in place and maintaining organized financial records ensures that you are always ready to submit an application. Over time, your track record and relationships can lead to faster approvals and better terms.

Deal structuring should also follow a consistent process. This includes determining the appropriate down payment, negotiating purchase terms, and ensuring that the deal meets

SBA requirements. By standardizing this process, you reduce the likelihood of errors and improve your efficiency. Each deal becomes easier as you refine your approach and apply lessons learned from previous transactions.

Closing and transition processes should also be systematized. This includes managing timelines, coordinating with all parties, and ensuring that all requirements are met. A clear checklist and timeline can help you navigate this phase smoothly and avoid delays. Once the property is acquired, having a structured plan for transition and setup ensures that your business operations continue without disruption.

Property management is another area where systems are essential. This includes maintenance schedules, budgeting processes, and performance tracking. By implementing systems for managing your properties, you can maintain their value, control expenses, and identify opportunities for improvement. Consistent management practices ensure that your properties remain strong assets over time.

Refinancing and growth strategies should also be part of your system. This includes regularly evaluating your properties for equity growth, monitoring market conditions, and identifying opportunities to leverage your assets. By incorporating these strategies into your system, you create a continuous cycle of growth that builds on itself over time. Another important element is team building. As your portfolio grows, you will need support from professionals such as lenders, brokers, attorneys, accountants, and property managers. Building a reliable team allows you to delegate tasks, reduce workload, and focus on strategic decisions. A strong team is a key component of a scalable system.

Documentation and organization are also critical. Keeping detailed records of your transactions, financials, and processes allows you to refine your system and improve over time. It also ensures that you are prepared for audits, refinancing, or future transactions. Organized documentation is the backbone of a professional and efficient operation.

Technology can enhance your system by automating tasks, tracking performance, and providing insights. Tools for financial management, property tracking, and communication can improve efficiency and reduce errors. Leveraging technology allows you to scale your operations without significantly increasing complexity.

Consistency is what turns a process into a system. By applying the same principles and steps repeatedly, you create predictability and reduce uncertainty. Each successful transaction reinforces your system and provides data that can be used to improve it further. Over time, this consistency leads to exponential growth.

Mindset is also a key factor in building a repeatable system. Viewing your real estate activities as a business rather than a series of individual deals changes how you approach decisions. It encourages discipline, strategic thinking, and long-term planning. This mindset is essential for sustaining growth and achieving your goals.

Ultimately, a repeatable system transforms SBA commercial real estate from a one-time opportunity into a scalable wealth-building engine. It allows you to move from reactive decision-making to proactive strategy, creating a pathway to consistent success.

Real-Life Math Example: Scaling Through a Repeatable System

Let's walk through a detailed real-life scenario to illustrate how a repeatable system can drive long-term growth. Consider a business owner named Elena who starts with a single owner-occupied property purchased for $900,000 using an SBA loan with a 10% down payment of $90,000. Her loan amount is $810,000 at 7% interest over 25 years, resulting in a monthly payment of approximately $5,720.

Elena develops a system for acquiring and managing properties. Every three years, she evaluates her property for equity growth and refinancing opportunities. After three years, her property appreciates to approximately $980,000, and she has paid down her loan balance to $770,000. This gives her $210,000 in equity.

She refinances and extracts $100,000, which she uses as a down payment on a second property valued at $700,000. This property generates rental income of $5,000 per month, with a mortgage payment of $4,200, creating positive cash flow of $800 per month.

Elena repeats this process every three to four years. By year 10, she owns three properties with a combined value of approximately $2.5 million. Her total equity exceeds $800,000, and her rental income provides consistent cash flow.

By year 20, Elena's portfolio grows to five properties with a combined value of over $5 million. Her total equity exceeds $2 million, and her rental income exceeds $20,000 per month. Her original investment of $90,000 has been leveraged into a substantial portfolio.

Now compare this to a scenario where Elena only acquires one property and does not implement a system. While she would still build equity, her growth would be significantly slower, and she would not benefit from multiple income streams. This example demonstrates how a repeatable system can transform a single investment into a scalable portfolio. By applying consistent processes, leveraging equity, and reinvesting strategically, business owners can achieve significant growth over time.

The key takeaway is that success in SBA commercial real estate is not about individual deals—it is about building a system that works repeatedly. With the right approach, discipline, and strategy, you can create a pathway to long-term wealth and financial independence.

Chapter 15

Mastering the Mindset and Discipline for Long-Term SBA Commercial Real Estate Success

At the highest level of success in SBA owner-occupied commercial real estate, the differentiating factor is no longer just knowledge, access to capital, or deal structure—it is mindset and discipline. While the strategies, systems, and financial tools you have learned throughout this series are powerful, they only produce results when applied consistently over time. The ability to think long-term, remain disciplined during uncertainty, and execute with clarity is what ultimately separates those who build lasting wealth from those who stall or fall short.

The first principle of a winning mindset is long-term thinking. Commercial real estate, especially when financed through SBA programs, is designed for stability and gradual growth. It is not a short-term flip strategy—it is a long-term wealth-building vehicle. Every payment, every improvement, and every strategic decision contributes to a larger outcome that unfolds over years, not months. Understanding this allows you to stay focused and avoid being distracted by short-term fluctuations or temporary challenges.

Patience is closely tied to long-term thinking. Many business owners expect immediate results, but real estate rewards consistency over time. Appreciation, equity growth, and income stability all develop gradually. Patience allows you to stay committed to your strategy even when progress feels slow. It also prevents impulsive decisions that can disrupt your long-term plan. The ability to wait, observe, and act strategically is one of the most valuable traits you can develop.

Discipline is the engine that drives success. This includes financial discipline, such as maintaining reserves, controlling expenses, and avoiding unnecessary debt. It also includes operational discipline, such as managing your property effectively, maintaining it properly, and staying organized. Discipline ensures that you follow through on your plans and make decisions based on logic rather than emotion.

Consistency is another key element. Success in SBA commercial real estate is not achieved through one perfect deal—it is achieved through repeated execution of sound strategies. Each property, each refinance, and each decision builds on the previous one. Consistency creates momentum, and momentum leads to exponential growth over time. By committing to consistent action, you turn your strategy into a reliable system.

Another important mindset shift is viewing challenges as opportunities. Every property will present issues, whether it is maintenance, financing, or market changes. Instead of seeing these challenges as setbacks, successful investors view them as opportunities to learn, improve, and strengthen their position. This perspective allows you to remain proactive and solution-oriented, rather than reactive and discouraged.

Risk awareness is also essential. While growth is important, it must be balanced with risk management. Understanding your limits, maintaining reserves, and avoiding overleveraging ensures that you can withstand challenges and continue growing. A disciplined approach to risk allows you to pursue opportunities without jeopardizing your stability.

Confidence plays a significant role in decision-making. Confidence is not about taking unnecessary risks—it is about trusting your knowledge, preparation, and strategy. As you gain experience, your confidence will grow, allowing you to make decisions more quickly and effectively. This confidence enables you to act when opportunities arise, rather than hesitating and missing them.

Another critical aspect is adaptability. Markets change, interest rates fluctuate, and business conditions evolve. Being able to adapt your strategy while maintaining your core principles is essential to long-term success. Flexibility allows you to navigate changes without losing direction, ensuring that your plan remains effective in different environments.

Focus is another key component. With so many opportunities and strategies available, it is easy to become distracted. Staying focused on your goals and your system ensures that your efforts are aligned and productive. This focus allows you to make progress steadily and avoid spreading yourself too thin.

Time management also plays a role in maintaining discipline. Balancing your business operations with your real estate activities requires careful planning and prioritization. Allocating time effectively ensures that both areas receive the attention they need to succeed.

Another important mindset is ownership. Taking full responsibility for your decisions, outcomes, and actions empowers you to improve and grow. Instead of blaming external factors, successful investors focus on what they can control and how they can improve. This sense of ownership drives continuous improvement and long-term success.

Vision is what ties everything together. Having a clear vision of what you want to achieve—whether it is financial independence, generational wealth, or business expansion—provides direction and motivation. This vision guides your decisions and keeps you aligned with your long-term goals.

Ultimately, mastering mindset and discipline is about creating a foundation that supports all your strategies and actions. It is what allows you to execute consistently, navigate challenges, and achieve lasting success in SBA commercial real estate.

Real-Life Math Example: The Power of Consistency and Discipline Over Time

Let's walk through a detailed real-life scenario to illustrate how mindset and discipline impact financial outcomes. Consider a business owner named Sophia who purchases an owner-occupied property for $1,000,000 using an SBA loan with a 10% down payment of $100,000. Her loan amount is $900,000 at 7% interest over 25 years, resulting in a monthly payment of approximately $6,360.

Sophia commits to a disciplined strategy. She sets aside $1,000 per month in reserves, maintains her property consistently, and evaluates her financial position annually. After five years, her property appreciates to approximately

$1,160,000, and her loan balance is reduced to $820,000, giving her $340,000 in equity.

Instead of spending her gains, Sophia reinvests. She refinances and extracts $120,000, which she uses as a down payment on a second property valued at $800,000. This property generates $6,000 per month in rental income, with a mortgage payment of $5,200, creating positive cash flow of $800 per month.

Sophia continues this disciplined approach. Every few years, she evaluates her portfolio, reinvests strategically, and maintains strong reserves. By year 15, she owns three properties with a combined value of approximately $3.5 million and equity exceeding $1.2 million.

Now consider the long-term impact. By year 25, Sophia's properties are largely paid off, and her portfolio is worth over $6 million, assuming consistent appreciation. Her rental income exceeds $25,000 per month, providing financial independence.

Now compare this to a scenario where Sophia lacks discipline. If she spends her equity, fails to maintain reserves, or overleverages, she may struggle with cash flow and miss opportunities to grow. Her portfolio may remain limited, and her financial progress may stall.

This example demonstrates how consistency, discipline, and long-term thinking can transform a single property into a powerful financial system. The strategies themselves are important, but it is the mindset behind them that determines success. By mastering your mindset and maintaining discipline, you create the foundation for everything you have learned in this series. This is what allows you to turn knowledge into action and action into lasting results.

Closing Thoughts

Turning Knowledge into Action and Building Your Future

As you reach the end of this book, it is important to recognize that what you now possess is far more than information—you have a complete framework for transforming your business, your finances, and your long-term future through owner-occupied SBA commercial real estate. You have learned how to move from tenant to owner, how to structure deals, how to qualify, how to acquire the right property, how to manage it effectively, and how to scale it into something much larger than a single investment. Most importantly, you have learned how to think differently—how to shift from short-term survival to long-term strategy.

The journey from leasing to ownership is one of the most powerful transitions a business owner can make. Renting is an expense that disappears every month, while ownership is an investment that compounds over time. This simple shift in direction changes everything. Instead of building someone else's wealth, you begin building your own. Instead of being subject to rent increases and external decisions, you gain control over your environment and your financial future. This control is not just financial—it is strategic, allowing you to align your business operations with your long-term goals.

Throughout this series, you have seen how SBA financing creates a unique opportunity. It lowers the barrier to entry, making ownership accessible even to those who may not have large amounts of capital. It provides long-term, manageable payments that support cash flow. It allows you to acquire an asset that appreciates, generates equity, and creates opportunities. When used correctly, it becomes more than a loan—it becomes a tool for transformation.

However, knowledge alone is not enough. The true value of everything you have learned lies in your ability to take action. There will always be reasons to wait—market uncertainty, interest rates, timing concerns, or fear of making the wrong decision. But the reality is that progress requires movement. The business owners who succeed are not those who wait for perfect conditions; they are those who prepare, act, learn, and adjust. Each step forward builds experience, confidence, and momentum.

It is also important to understand that this journey is not about perfection. There will be challenges, unexpected costs, and decisions that could have been made differently. These are not failures—they are part of the process. Every experienced investor has faced obstacles, and those experiences are what refine their strategy and strengthen their approach. The goal is not to avoid every mistake, but to make informed decisions, manage risk, and continue moving forward.

As you move ahead, your first step is to evaluate your current position. Look at your business, your financials, and your readiness for ownership. Identify what needs to be improved, whether it is your credit, your reserves, or your financial organization. Begin building relationships with lenders, brokers, and professionals who can support your journey. Start analyzing properties, even if you are not ready to buy immediately. This preparation lays the foundation for action.

Your first property is not the end goal—it is the beginning. It is the foundation upon which everything else is built. Once you acquire your first owner-occupied property, your perspective will change. You will begin to see opportunities differently, understand leverage more clearly, and recognize the potential for growth. Each step after that becomes easier because you are building on experience and success.

Over time, this process can evolve into something much larger. Your property becomes an asset that supports your business, generates income, and builds equity. That equity can be leveraged to acquire additional properties, creating multiple income streams and accelerating your financial growth. What starts as a single decision—to stop renting and start owning—can lead to a portfolio of assets that provide stability, freedom, and opportunity.

It is also important to keep your long-term vision in focus. Whether your goal is financial independence, business expansion, or creating generational wealth, your real estate strategy should align with that vision. Every decision you make—every property you acquire, every refinance you execute, every improvement you make—should move you closer to that goal. This alignment ensures that your efforts are purposeful and that your progress is meaningful.

Discipline will be your greatest ally. Maintaining reserves, managing your properties effectively, and making strategic decisions consistently will determine your long-term success. It is not the size of your first deal that matters most—it is your ability to execute your strategy over time. Consistency creates momentum, and momentum creates results.

Another key takeaway is the importance of thinking beyond yourself. The wealth you build through commercial real estate has the potential to impact not only your life but also the lives of your family and future generations. By planning strategically, educating those who will follow you, and structuring your assets effectively, you can create a legacy that extends far beyond your own efforts. This is where real estate becomes more than an investment—it becomes a foundation for lasting impact. As you reflect on everything you have learned, remember that the opportunity in front of you is significant. SBA owner-occupied commercial real estate is not just a niche strategy—it is a proven pathway used by countless business owners to build wealth, stability, and independence. The difference between those who succeed and those who do not is not access to information—it is the willingness to act, adapt, and persist.

There will never be a perfect time to begin. There will always be variables you cannot control. But what you can control is your preparation, your mindset, and your actions. Start where you are. Take the first step. Build momentum. Each decision you make moves you closer to your goals.

In the end, this journey is about more than property ownership. It is about taking control of your financial future, aligning your business with your long-term vision, and creating opportunities that extend beyond what you once thought possible. It is about turning effort into equity, strategy into stability, and knowledge into lasting success.

The path is now clear. The tools are in your hands. The next move is yours.

How to Get a Personalized SBA Commercial Mortgage Review

If you found this book helpful, you may want to see how these strategies apply to your specific financial situation.

SBA commercial mortgage financing is highly customized—your business income, financial statements, credit profile, property type, industry, and long-term goals all play a role in determining what you qualify for and how your loan should be structured.

Every borrower's situation is different. Your revenue trends, business model, tax returns, debt obligations, ownership structure, and the type of commercial property you are purchasing, refinancing, or building all impact your options. The strategies and examples in this book are designed to teach you how SBA commercial mortgage loans work—but your actual loan approval, terms, and structure can only be determined by analyzing your real financial profile.

If you would like a no-obligation SBA Commercial Mortgage review, you can request one here:

Email: info@FinibiMortgage.com

A licensed mortgage broker will review your business financials, income structure, credit profile, and goals, and explain what SBA financing options may be available to you—including:

• SBA 7(a) commercial mortgage loans• SBA 504 fixed-rate commercial real estate financing• Owner-occupied property qualification strategies• Business acquisition with real estate financing• Commercial refinance and cash-out strategies• Construction and expansion loan structuring• Advanced SBA deal structuring to maximize approval

No cost. No pressure. No obligation.

Sincerely,

Joseph G. Correa

Finibi Mortgage Inc.

Licensed Mortgage Broker

About the Author

Joseph G. Correa is a licensed mortgage broker and the founder of Finibi Mortgage, a Florida-based brokerage specializing in SBA commercial mortgage loans, non-QM lending, and strategic real estate financing solutions for business owners, entrepreneurs, and investors.

With more than two decades of experience in mortgage lending, underwriting, and deal structuring, Joseph has helped thousands of clients secure financing for commercial real estate, business acquisitions, and complex transactions using both traditional and alternative lending strategies.

Unlike traditional loan officers who focus only on basic qualification, Joseph's approach emphasizes **cash flow analysis, deal structuring, and strategic financing**. He believes that business owners should not be limited by rigid lending formulas, but instead empowered by understanding how to structure deals that align with lender guidelines and maximize approval potential.

Joseph is widely recognized for his expertise in:

• SBA 7(a) and SBA 504 commercial mortgage loans• Owner-occupied commercial real estate financing• Business acquisition with real estate structuring• Commercial refinance and cash flow optimization• Construction and expansion financing• Advanced loan structuring and approval strategy

Through his education platform, Finibi Academy, Joseph has trained tens of thousands of students worldwide in mortgage strategy, real estate investing, credit optimization, and financial independence.

He created the *SBA Commercial Mortgage Loan Mastery Series* to provide a clear, step-by-step roadmap for borrowers and professionals who want to understand, qualify for, and scale commercial real estate using SBA financing.

His mission is simple:

To help business owners use strategic financing to acquire assets, build cash flow, and create long-term wealth.

When he is not structuring loans or writing, Joseph works with clients across the United States to design customized SBA financing strategies aligned with their business goals and growth plans.

The SBA Commercial Mortgage Loan Mastery Series Roadmap

The Complete Guide to Using SBA Financing to Build Commercial Real Estate and Business Wealth

The purpose of *The SBA Commercial Mortgage Loan Mastery Series* is to give business owners, investors, and mortgage professionals the exact strategies used by lenders and underwriters—translated into simple, practical steps you can apply in real life.

This series takes you from beginner to advanced mastery of how to qualify, structure, and scale commercial real estate and business financing using SBA mortgage loans.

Each book builds on the last. You are not just learning how to get approved—you are learning how to control your approvals and scale your opportunities.

Book 1 — SBA Commercial Mortgage Loan Fundamentals Understand how SBA mortgage programs work, including 7(a) and 504 loans, and how to qualify.

Book 2 — Getting Approved for an SBA Commercial Mortgage Loan Learn step-by-step strategies to meet lender requirements and secure funding.

Book 3 — Owner-Occupied Property Financing with SBA Loans Learn how to buy or refinance your business property using SBA financing.

Book 4 — Buying a Business and Real Estate with SBA Financing Acquire a business and its property in one structured transaction.

Book 5 — SBA 7(a) Mortgage Loan Strategies Master flexible loan structures for business and real estate funding.

Book 6 — SBA 504 Mortgage Loans for Commercial Real Estate Use long-term fixed-rate financing for large property acquisitions.

Book 7 — Refinancing Commercial Debt with SBA Loans Lower payments, improve cash flow, and restructure existing debt.

Book 8 — SBA Loans for Construction and Expansion Build, renovate, and scale commercial properties with structured financing.

Book 9 — SBA Loan Requirements, Rates, and Structures Understand how to compare options and choose the best loan.

Book 10 — Advanced SBA Commercial Mortgage Structuring Engineer approvals and maximize leverage using expert strategies.

This series is designed to move you from:

Understanding → Execution → Scaling → Mastery

By the end, you will not just know how to qualify—you will know how to structure, analyze, and scale deals like a professional.

Educational & Financial Disclaimer

The *SBA Commercial Mortgage Loan Mastery Series* is intended for educational and informational purposes only.

This content is designed to help readers understand SBA commercial mortgage lending, real estate financing strategies, and business acquisition concepts. It is not financial, legal, tax, or investment advice.

Joseph G. Correa and Live Stronger Faster are not acting as your personal financial advisor, attorney, accountant, or mortgage professional through this publication.

SBA loan programs, underwriting guidelines, interest rates, and lender requirements may change at any time and vary by lender.

All examples in this series are for illustration purposes only and do not guarantee approval or results.

Always consult with licensed professionals before making financial decisions.

Risk Disclosure

SBA commercial mortgage lending and real estate investing involve risk.

Business performance, income stability, interest rate changes, market conditions, and lender guidelines can all impact loan approval and financial outcomes.

Borrowing against real estate or using leverage increases both potential returns and risk.

Failure to repay a loan may result in foreclosure and loss of property.

Cash flow, rental income, appreciation, and business performance are not guaranteed.

All strategies presented in this series are educational and must be evaluated based on your individual financial situation.

You are solely responsible for your financial decisions.

www.ingramcontent.com/pod-product-compliance
Ingram Content Group UK Ltd.
Pitfield, Milton Keynes, MK11 3LW, UK
UKHW020159290926
15471UKWH00005B/951

9 798295 817748